The Elegant Essay

Teacher's Manual

Lesha Myers, M.Ed.

Third Edition, March 2011 Institute for Excellence in Writing, L.L.C.

Also by Lesha Myers:
The Elegant Essay: Building Blocks for Analytical Writing (Student Book)
Windows to the World: An Introduction to Literary Analysis
Writing Research Papers: The Essential Tools

Copyright Policy

The Elegant Essay
Building Blocks for Analytical Writing
Copyright © 2006 Lesha Myers
Third Edition, 2011
Third Printing version 2, May 2013

ISBN 978-1-62341-001-8

Every effort has been made to contact copyright holders and students for permission to reproduce borrowed material. We regret any oversights that may have occurred.

Unless otherwise noted, all Bible verses are from the King James Version.

Institute for Excellence in Writing
8799 N. 387 Road
Locust Grove, OK 74352
800.856.5815
info@iew.com
IEW.com

Printed in the United States of America

Accessing Your Download

The purchase of this book entitles its owner to a free download of the *Elegant Essay* e-resources: *Developing the Essayist* audio download, TEE Essay Planning Sheets, and TEE Third Edition Calendar.

To download your supplemental resources, please follow the directions below:

1. Go to our website, IEW.com
2. Sign in to your online customer account. If you do not have an account, you will need to create one.
3. After you are logged in, go to this web page: IEW.com/TEE-E
4. Click on the red download arrow.
5. You will be taken to your File Downloads page. Click on the file name, and the e-book will download onto your computer.

Please note: You are free to download and print this e-book resource as many times as needed for use within *your immediate family or classroom*. However, this information is proprietary, and we are trusting you to be on your honor not to share it with anyone. Thank you.

If you have any difficulty receiving this download after going through the steps above, please call 800.856.5815.

Institute for Excellence in Writing
8799 N. 387 Road
Locust Grove, OK 74352

Table of Contents

Thank you!

I am extremely indebted to Jill Pike, Pamela White, and Maria Gerber for providing such excellent feedback, editing, and ideas for this revision. Their comments have been invaluable, especially their attention to detail.

Please visit our websites:
Lesha Myers
Cameron-Publishing.com
Click on *The Elegant Essay.*

Institute for Excellence in Writing
excellenceinwriting.com

Foreword

In 2008, I was graced with the privilege of meeting Lesha Myers at the Writing Educator's Symposium in Murrieta, California. Attending her "Arts of Arguing" session, I marveled at her passion for teaching and her desire to help students and teachers excel in their writing efforts. Her superb courses, *The Elegant Essay* and *Windows to the World: An Introduction to Literary Analysis*, were blessings to my family and became proven resources for many families working on advanced writing instruction.

My students and I enjoyed getting to know Lesha through her fine work. In her warm, friendly writing style, Lesha reveals much of herself as she gently guides her reader through the processes necessary to craft words in essays and intelligently explore and write on literature. Additionally, the teaching tools she suggested have helped me become a better teacher across the curriculum.

In 2011, I was privileged to serve as Lesha's project manager for *Writing Research Papers: The Essential Tools.* As the book was coming close to publication, Lesha confided that she was battling against cancer. Facing the storm with exceptional courage, she desired to die well so as to glorify her Lord and Savior. She did. Instead of letting the disease dictate her days, she continued teaching until the end of the school year, expressing a strong and genuine faith to the many communities she served. Lesha passed from this life on June 29, 2012.

I am grateful for all that Lesha Myers has provided for teachers and young writers. I pray that you too will enjoy getting to know her as you study her materials. Throughout her books, Lesha often invites students to contact her and share what they are learning. Please do! To continue her legacy we have assembled a team of like-minded teachers to respond to your comments and questions. You may reach them using Lesha's email address: Lesha@excellenceinwriting.com.

Blessings,
Jill Pike
Accomplished Instructor with
The Institute for Excellence in Writing

TEACHING HELPS

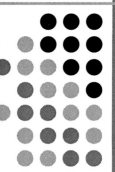

Course Overview

Contents

The Elegant Essay course teaches middle and high school students the *form* of essay writing, that is, the basic structure or format or organization that undergirds all types of essays. Before they tackle this course, students should be able to write an understandable paragraph with a topic and clincher sentence.

Course topics include the following:
1. Thesis statement
2. Essay organization
3. Transitions
4. Introductions
5. Conclusions
6. Advanced thesis statements and planning charts
7. Descriptive practice essay
8. Persuasive practice essay

In addition to form or structure, writing includes four other components: ideas, style, mechanics, and voice. Although all of these are important, and sometimes we address them, they are not the focus of this introductory course.

Materials Needed

The student book contains all the handouts needed for the class. The teacher may make copies of selected pages from the teacher's book if needed for students.

Student Samples

I am grateful that some of my students have given me permission to share their work. Consequently, I have included authentic student samples throughout the lessons; however, I have corrected all mechanical errors and sometimes made additional modifications.

Schedule

The Elegant Essay is adaptable from a 4-week crash course (which I call Essay Boot Camp) to a 13 - 16 week basic course. Two sample schedules are included.

Teaching Strategy

The *Elegant Essay* course relies on a four-step teaching strategy:

- **Preliminary Instruction**—Each lesson begins with *instruction* in the students' book, which speaks directly to the student, that you might use in a variety of ways. First, you might present the material in the sections orally, and then ask your students to read it on their own, perhaps as homework. Second, you might read the sections along with your students, stopping for explanation and clarification as needed. Third, you might ask the students to read it on their own ahead of time, and then focus on specific areas. I've experienced success with all methods.

- **Modeling**—After the initial instruction, *model* each lesson's concept for your student(s). Lead him through the assignment, allowing him to contribute where he can; however, don't be concerned if you are presenting most of the ideas. The idea behind the modeling step is to demonstrate the skills—how to write a thesis statement, for example. Lessons labeled "modeling" on the following pages are included to help you with this process. Additionally, the completed models are reprinted in the Chapter 4 Note Page of the student text.

- **Practice with Help**—Next, allow your students to *practice* the ideas you've introduced, giving help where needed. This could be in groups if you are teaching a class, with a sibling if the two are close in age, or with you. If you are the partner, you will need to exercise some restraint and allow your student to take the lead, providing help only where needed. Each chapter contains two sets of student exercises. The first lesson is designed to be used for this step.

- **On Your Own**—Unless students can perform the skills on their own, they haven't mastered them. The second set of exercises in each lesson is designed to be completed independently or as homework. Review students' work and offer additional instruction as needed. Make sure your students understand each lesson—how to write an introduction, for instance—but don't expect mastery. They will have ample time to practice as they move on to writing actual elegant essays.

All of the lessons have been designed to facilitate the teacher who believes writing is not his or her strength. In fact, most of the parents of my writing students as well as classroom teachers say their own writing skills have improved as they work alongside their students. In the section on Lesson Plans, I've included a short list of lesson-specific problems I encounter as I teach these lessons.

For more information and discussion on this teaching strategy, see the section on Teaching Methods.

Grading & Evaluation

Too many times we evaluate our students prematurely before they have time to practice and internalize the concepts we teach them. Since this course introduces basic essay-writing concepts, I believe that students should have more time to practice them before being rated on their performance and that formal evaluation should not occur until near the end of this course.

Two ways of grading students are discussed in the Grading Methods section of these teacher pages: a Checklist Method and a Point System. If you like either, feel free to use them, but keep in mind that you are also entirely free to devise your own system that meets your personal course objectives.

For more information on grading and evaluation, see the section on Grading Methods.

Course Schedule

For a Homeschool Co-op

I have used several schedules to teach the content of this course. When I teach homeschoolers, my class meets one day a week for two hours, and I teach an entire chapter during those two hours. Students separate into small groups and complete the practice exercises; then we regroup and I offer further instruction as necessary. I assign homework, which students submit to me by email two or three days before the next class meets. This gives me time to review and comment on their work and decide whether to reteach or move on. A sample schedule for a co-op class follows.

For a Classroom

When I teach in the classroom, I teach these chapters along with some literature. That gives me time to review students' work and grade it if necessary before tackling the next essay topic. Sometimes I devote an entire class period to an elegant essay chapter. At other times, I teach shorter lessons and intersperse them with my lessons on the literature. To develop a schedule for the classroom, use the sample co-op schedule, and teach each chapter over the course of the week. For example, you might do the following:

Day 1: Review homework/independent practice
Day 2: Model/instruct
Day 3: Practice with Help (group work)
Day 4: Catch up or reteach as necessary

For Essay Boot Camp

I've also taught these lessons over the course of three or four weeks in a concentrated way I call Essay Boot Camp. I've done this at the beginning of an honors-level 10th grade class and at the beginning of a 12th grade composition class. Although the students in these classes had some skill in essay writing, they just needed a bit of a refresher, so we were able to cover the ground pretty quickly. In both of these cases, I omitted the descriptive essay. A sample schedule for Essay Boot Camp follows.

The Elegant Essay Schedule for a Weekly Co-op Class

Ch.	In Class	Homework *Complete Before Class*
1	As needed, introduce yourself, the students, and your procedures. Optional: If students have not worked together before, you might conduct some kind of icebreaker. Google "Classroom Icebreakers" for ideas. Optional: If desired, review any previously taught techniques. These might include the IEW Basic Essay Model and IEW style techniques (sentence openers/dress-ups/decorations). See Appendix C. Introduce *The Elegant Essay* book, especially its structure and format. Teach Chapter 1—Essay Overview.	
2	Pop Quiz or Entry Card Discuss kinds of essays and their resulting thesis statements. Model how to create thesis statements for each. Group students (3 - 4 each) and give them practice generating theses using Exercise 1. Be sure to leave time to discuss students' work and share it or One Class's Answers to Exercise 1.	Read TEE Chapter 2.
3a	*Note: This chapter is designed to take two weeks. If your student has had plenty of essay practice, you could do it in one, but I don't recommend it.* <u>Week 1</u> Pop Quiz or Entry Card Go over and then collect Exercise 2. Address issues. Share exemplary models from the students' answers or One Class's Answers to Exercise 2. Model the simple structure and discuss its use and limitations. Model telling vs. showing. Practice with class using sentences provided. Teach and model the first three kinds of evidence and support for body paragraphs: example, personal experience, statistics. Group students, assign Exercise 3a, and give them something to write their paragraph on (chart paper, transparency). When complete, the class should evaluate each group's paragraph: ➤ Is the paragraph understandable? Good topic, clincher, and flow? ➤ Does the evidence support the assertion? ➤ What is done well? ➤ What might be improved? Assign Exercise 4a. Students should practice writing body paragraphs for the first three evidence/support methods only.	Exercise 2 Read TEE Chapter 3. <u>To do ahead of time:</u> Find articles that contain statistics on courage, gifts, women in the military, or education. Students will need these statistics to write their practice body paragraphs. Alternatively, you might allow students to make up some statistics for this exercise only. Discuss how unethical that would be in an authentic situation.

Ch.	In Class	Homework *Complete Before Class*
3b	<u>Week 2</u> Pop Quiz or Entry Card Discuss students' body paragraphs created for Exercise 4a. Address issues. Share exemplary models from the students' answers or One Class's Answer to Exercise 4a. Teach & model the remaining five kinds of evidence and support for body paragraphs: research/expert testimony, observation, description, anecdote, analogy. Group students, assign Exercise 3b, and give them something to write their paragraph on (chart paper, transparency). When complete, the class should evaluate each group's paragraph: ➤ Is the paragraph understandable? Good topic, clincher, and flow? ➤ Does the evidence support the assertion? ➤ What is done well? ➤ What might be improved? Assign Exercise 4b for independent practice. Students should practice writing body paragraphs for the remaining evidence/support methods.	Exercise 4a, choosing from the first three kinds of evidence: example, personal experience, statistics. **<u>To do ahead of time:</u>** Find articles that contain research on courage, gifts, women in the military, or education. Students will need these statistics to write their practice body paragraphs. Alternatively, you might allow students to make up some statistics for this exercise only. Discuss how unethical that would be in an authentic situation.
4	Pop Quiz or Entry Card Discuss students' body paragraphs created for Exercise 4b. Address issues. Share exemplary models from the students' answers. Teach and model yellow line and road sign transitions. Group students, give them the sentence strips from Exercise 5, and have them create a paragraph with transitions. Share and discuss. Use One Class's Answer to Exercise 5 as needed. Assign Exercise 6 for independent practice.	Complete Exercise 4b, choosing two of the remaining five types of support. Read TEE Chapter 4. **<u>To do ahead of time:</u>** Copy and cut transition sentence strips.
5	Pop Quiz or Entry Card Discuss students' paragraphs created for Exercise 6. Address issues. Share exemplary models from the students' answers or One Class's Answer to Exercise 6. Teach each of the dramatic openings and introductory methods using the examples in the student pages and models. Break up into groups and complete Exercise 7. Have each group do all or a subset of the types. Share, discuss, and provide clarification where necessary. Assign Exercise 8 for independent practice.	Complete Exercise 6. Read TEE Chapter 5.

The Elegant Essay Teacher's Manual   9 ● ● ●

Ch.	In Class	Homework *Complete Before Class*
6	Pop Quiz or Entry Card Discuss students' paragraphs created for Exercise 6. Address issues. Share exemplary models from the students' answers or One Class's Answer to Exercise 8. Teach the basic conclusion technique, and model it for both narrative and persuasive genres. Have groups try it with Exercise 9, and share the One Class's Answer as desired. Teach and model the seven conclusion techniques. Emphasize the importance of framing. Group students, and ask them to practice creating conclusions using Exercise 10. Share examples from One Class's Answers to Exercise 10. Assign Exercise 11 for independent practice.	Complete Exercise 8. Read TEE Chapter 6.
7	Discuss students' paragraphs created for Exercise 11. Address issues. Share exemplary models from the students' answers or One Class's Answer to Exercise 11. Review the form of an essay and the various pieces: evidence, transitions, introduction, conclusion. Reteach as necessary. Return to Chapter 4 and teach/review the bridge transition. Model how to turn Spurgeon's devotion into an essay. Have students write the essay in Exercise 12 individually in class. When complete, have them share first in pairs and then as a class. Assign Exercise 13 for independent practice.	Complete Exercise 11. Read TEE Chapter 7. **To do ahead of time:** Make sure students have access to dictionaries in case they need to look up some of the words in Spurgeon's devotion.
8	*This chapter is scheduled for one week, but depending on how much practice your students have with planning charts, you may wish to add an additional week.* Pop Quiz or Entry Card Discuss students' essays created for Exercise 13. Address issues. Share exemplary models from the students' answers or One Class's Answer to Exercise 13. Teach and model advanced thesis statements. Group students and have them do a thesis workshop using Exercise 14. Share results on the whiteboard or chart paper. Discuss discrepancies using One Class's Answers to Exercise 14 as needed. Assign Exercise 15 for independent practice as necessary.	Complete Exercise 13. Read TEE Chapter 8. **To do ahead of time:** In preparation for the persuasive essay in Ch. 10, you might conduct some research and gather some sources for students to use related to the prompt, "Is the Internet a hero or a villain?"

Ch.	In Class	Homework *Complete Before Class*
(8)	*Optional Week, As Needed* Introduce the planning charts, and model with the two narrative paragraphs provided. Group students and have them do Exercise 16. Assign Exercise 17 for independent practice.	Complete Exercise 15.
9a	Review the process for writing a descriptive essay. Choose topics; begin outlining using the form of choice. See the sequence of teaching steps in the lesson plans.	Complete Exercise 15 or 17. Read TEE Chapter 9. Work on first draft.
9b	Writing Workshop: Work on essays. Do thesis workshop or peer reviews, as desired. <u>Note</u>: You may need a third week for this chapter.	Finish essay. Read TEE Chapter 10.
10a	Review the process for a persuasive paper. Do Exercise 18 (Internet thesis workshop) in class. See the sequence of steps in the lesson plans. Briefly discuss MLA citation. For free MLA guidance, see http://owl.english.purdue.edu/owl/resource/747/01/.	Complete research. Work on first draft.
10b	Discuss methods of citing research. Continue working on papers with peers. <u>Note</u>: You may need a third week for this chapter.	Finish essay.

The Elegant Essay Schedule for Essay Boot Camp

Three- or Four-Week Schedule

You probably won't be able to teach elegant essay concepts in fewer than three weeks, and even then, the three-week schedule is extremely aggressive. Both you and your students will need to be focused, and you will need to make sure you have plenty of time to grade, evaluate, and offer feedback.

If you feel this schedule is too aggressive, you might add five days and expand it to four weeks. Add days near introductions and conclusions, a day to evaluate the form review in Chapter 7, a day for the persuasive essays (descriptive essay is omitted for Essay Boot Camp), and two others when you need them.

Elegant Essay Boot Camp Schedule				
Day	**Chapter**	**Lessons**		
		Instruction & Modeling	Practice with Help	On Your Own
1	1-Overview	Introduction		
1	2-Thesis Statements	Reading/Modeling		
2	2-Thesis Statements	Group Practice	Exercise 1	Exercise 2
3	3-Essay Organization	SEE and Showing vs. Telling		
4	3-Essay Organization	Model example, personal experience, statistics	Exercise 3a	Exercise 4a
5	3-Essay Organization	Model remaining types of support	Exercise 3b	Exercise 4b
6	4-Transitions	Model transitions	Exercise 5	Exercise 6
7	5-Introductions	Model introductions	Exercise 7	Exercise 8
8	6-Conclusions	Model conclusions	Exercise 9	Exercise 10
9	7-Form Review	Model form	Exercise 12	Exercise 13
10	8-Thesis Polishing	Model advanced thesis	Exercise 14	Exercise 15
11	10-Persuasive Essay	Reading/Thinking	Rough Draft	
12		Evaluate & reteach as necessary	Final Draft	
13	Wrap-Up/Evaluate	Begin planning next elegant essay.		

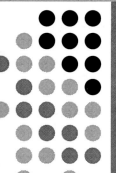

TEACHING METHODS

The overview section briefly introduced the teaching methodology and methods *The Elegant Essay* uses. This section discusses them in more detail and offers practical suggestions on how to use the methods in your classes.

Mini-Lectures

When you begin teaching, you will invariably begin with a mini-lecture to introduce the new material. The main thing to focus on with mini-lectures is to keep them *mini*—no more than 20 minutes. Students frequently lose concentration after this time and "zone out." Even if they appear to be listening attentively, their minds might be miles away. In writing, students do need direct instruction, and lectures are the most efficient way to deliver it, but they also need immediate opportunities to put what they've learned into practice. Ideally, lectures should be interspersed with frequent modeling and practice sessions.

Reading—Before or After?

With respect to assigning reading from *The Elegant Essay*, you have a choice to make: Will you assign it before or after the teaching session? Either way has merit. If you assign the reading before, students should be familiar with the material before you model it. (To encourage accountability and check for understanding, you might administer pop quizzes, discussed below.) Your lectures could be shorter, and you could concentrate on troublesome areas rather than teaching the concepts from scratch.

On the other hand, if you always go over the same material contained in *The Elegant Essay* at the beginning of each class, students will ask themselves why they should read ahead or why they should pay attention in class. They've already read and understood what you're teaching. In this case, it might be better to assign the reading after class, as review. This could also serve as extra reinforcement because students sometimes need to see information in a variety of forms over some period of time before they internalize it. Of course, you still might have an accountability issue.

You might try each method and see which works better for your students and situation.

Pop Quizzes & Entry Cards

I frequently administer either pop quizzes or entry cards at the beginning of class. The difference between the two is purpose. The quizzes act as incentives for students to come prepared for class. They provide accountability. Most of the time, I record quiz scores, and they become part of a student's grade. The exception is when the entire class bombs the quiz. This tells me that either my quiz question was confusing or that I need to revisit the skill I was testing. And because the students who earned a high score feel I'm not being fair to them if I ditch the scores, I return the papers and tell them if they earn a lower score on a subsequent quiz, they can exchange this score for the future one. Many questions are suggested for each chapter. Choose the ones you like—usually only one or two.

The procedure works this way:
- Quarter sheets of paper
- One or two short questions
- Collect papers or switch with another student
- Go over answers and perhaps correct in class

Suggestions for pop quiz questions appear in each chapter's lesson plan.

The procedure for entry cards is exactly the same, but the purpose is a little different. Recognizing that most students need time to internalize a new skill, I might ask for an entry card about a skill I taught yesterday or last week. For example, after teaching how to write a thesis statement in Chapter 2, on another day I might ask students to write a thesis statement for a particular writing genre and focus, or I might ask for an academic (three-pronged) thesis statement on a particular topic. After giving students a few minutes to think and write, I ask a few students to share their ideas. The class discusses these. I collect the entry cards because students don't feel the task is worth their effort if I don't, and glance over them. If I notice a particular difficulty, I address it.

Both the quizzes and the entry cards help me to know what has already been caught and what needs to be retaught.

Note-Taking

If you lecture, your students should be taking notes—always. The reason is not so much that what you are saying is important, although it is, but that the students are *engaged*. Research shows that even if students never look at their notes again, simply the act of taking them increases retention. Plus, for students who have difficulty maintaining focus, the ones who are easily distracted, taking notes helps keep their minds on the task at hand.

Note pages are included at the end of each chapter of the student book, right before the exercise pages. Because these include pre-printed headings, they will help students follow your mini-lecture's order. (If you skip a section, be sure to inform your students; otherwise they will get very confused!) Make sure students use these sheets. Force them if you have to. They should understand that note-taking is not optional.

You might meet resistance on two fronts. First, some students will say that note-taking is a "waste of time" because they already understand the material. In many cases, they are probably right. However, too many times I've seen students who relied on their memories and never devised a personal note-taking system fail miserably at higher educational levels. They never learned the skill. When they got to the point where they needed to use it, they couldn't. Second, some students will not know how to take notes. In that case, you need to teach them. How? By direct instruction ("Write that down") or modeling (demonstrating how to take notes on an overhead transparency, whiteboard, or easel) or following a model (look up Cornell Notes, for example).

If students need incentives and accountability to take notes, you might give it to them in a couple of different forms. First, monitor your class. Students who aren't taking notes should be gently reminded to do so. Second, periodically collect notes, especially at the beginning of the course when you are teaching this skill/procedure. Look them over, briefly, and address any difficulties. Grade them if that seems appropriate. Third, give periodic open-note quizzes where students can use their own notes but nothing else to answer quiz questions. Remember that you are building a skill (and a procedure). Once students have grasped it, you can back off on the accountability, or you might have to return to it briefly now and then just for reinforcement.

Modeling

Modeling is another word for demonstrating the steps involved in completing a particular skill. It's an extremely important part of teaching that overlaps your lectures. Yes, you want to *tell* your students about the skill ("The thesis statement gives form to an essay's ideas and helps readers to follow your thoughts."), but you also want to *show* them how to do it ("These are the steps you take to write a thesis statement. First, . . .").

Think Aloud

Some students will quickly catch on to whatever you are teaching. They will intuitively grasp the concept. Most will not however, especially in an area such as writing. They need step-by-step instruction. For them (and also for the intuitive learner who may not know *why* they know), you need to model your internal thinking, and one way to do this is by expressing your thoughts out loud.

For example, let's say you want to think of support for the idea that books are better than movies. You might think out loud and say something like this:

> Well let's see. I know that when I support an idea I need proof. And I've learned that I can draw on several different areas for .that proof or evidence. [Note that you need to use academic words such as *support, proof,* or *evidence.*] These are [Write them on the board in a column as you say them] examples, personal experience, statistics, research, observation, description, anecdote, and analogy.

> Well, I certainly don't want to do any research [Cross off research.], so let me think about the others. [Pause and look like you're thinking.]

> Hmmm. I'm going to consider personal experience because that seems like the easiest for this situation. Have I ever seen a movie that I was really disappointed in, especially after reading the book? Yes! There was *Charly* with Cliff Robertson, which I saw after reading *Flowers for Algernon*. There was so much the movie left out! Plus, when it showed the technology center, those computers were so old they belonged in a museum. [Write "*Charly*—incomplete & antiquated" next to personal experience on the white-board.] I could use compare *Charly* and *Flowers for Algernon* and use that as proof or evidence. [Use academic words again.]

> I wonder if I can think of another example. Hmmm. [Pause.] After reading *To Kill a Mockingbird*, we saw the movie with Gregory Peck. The students in my English class [or group] said there were some scenes they liked better in the movie than in the book, like when Atticus guarded Tom Robinson at the jail. [Write "TKAMB—jail scene" on the board.]. But that might not work because it doesn't support my idea that books are better than movies. [Write some question marks after your note on the board—"???." Remember that it's important to demonstrate ideas that do and don't work out to teach students how to evaluate their own.]

You could continue, and if you were actually teaching this lesson, you would want to go through all the other areas, either thinking of proof that would work or saying something like, "I can't think of anything for this one right now," and drawing a dash next to it. But for purposes of how a think aloud works, we've done enough.

A couple of things are very important to do when you model. First, make sure you go through all of the skill steps in an orderly fashion, even if you think they seem obvious. You are building pathways in your students' brains, and if you make too big of a leap from one concept to the next, all of your effort will be lost. You must also write your thoughts down on an overhead, whiteboard, easel, or for a very small class, a piece of paper that everyone can see. This is extremely important because students will process what you tell/show them at different rates, and some students don't comprehend well what they hear orally. Seeing and hearing the concepts helps all students learn.

A couple of side notes: I have some perceptual motor difficulties, and it's very difficult for me to write on the whiteboard at the same time that I'm teaching or thinking. But I know students need this information in a visual form, so I've learned to compensate in two ways. Either I prepare my think aloud ahead of time (prewritten on an easel, PowerPoint slide, or overhead transparency), and then reveal a section at a time, or I ask a student to be my scribe and write my thoughts on the board. I explain to students why I do this, and that builds some camaraderie, especially with those who have academic difficulties. Plus it makes me seem more real rather than a know-it-all teacher. Second, I don't always have access to large whiteboards, overheads, LCD projectors, or other expensive equipment, and small whiteboards or easels don't always work, so I've found an inexpensive alternative: shower board from hardware stores. In the plumbing section, you will find very large boards (4' x 8') used to line shower stalls. You can write on these with a whiteboard marker, and although they won't last as long as the "real deal," they will do in a pinch. If you find it hard to get such a large board into your car, you can ask the store to cut it for you (They might charge for the cut.) into two 2' x 8' or two 4' x 4' sections.

Modeling Helps

Because it is difficult to come up with modeling ideas on the spot, I've provided some suggestions on how to model each lesson. Keep in mind that these are only suggestions, and you (or your students) can probably come up with more and better ideas. I've tried to provide more modeling ideas than you will need, so you can use one (or two) ideas for the initial modeling and the remainder for reviewing or reteaching. All of the models are reprinted in Appendix A of the student book; that way students can follow along, or if a student misses your class, he or she will have a way to catch up.

Segue to Practice

It's a good idea to overlap the modeling and practice steps and whenever possible to have your class think along with you. For example, in the above demonstration of the think aloud procedure, you might say something like, "I can't think of an analogy. Can any of you?" When students offer their own ideas, be sure to praise them. If it's an "off" example, gently correct and see if you can still use the idea. For example, "I'm not seeing how that's an analogy because I don't see the comparison between the two similar ideas, but that would make an excellent observation. Let's record it in that category. [Write it down.] It's a good one—thank you for sharing it." If you don't treat students' suggestions with respect, they won't offer them. And you want them to participate, to start thinking, and to be ready to do the next step with others.

Practice with Help

Have you ever been in the situation where you've listened to someone explain how to do something and understood, but when you went to do it on your own, you completely messed up? We all have. We can listen to explanations all day, but until we can perform the action on our own, we haven't learned. The Practice with Help step allows students to combine their brains with others' to practice the skill. You should move to this step once you feel students have understood your modeling in general, but before they have complete understanding.

Grouping Methods

There's been a lot written on how to group students and how to ensure that everyone participates. Should the groups be the same—all the same skill level (low, medium, and high groups), the same gender, the same interest? Or should they be diversified? Should students decide who to work with, should you, or should this be random? I've tried all of these methods, and use all of them from time to time, but the one I like the best is random, or at least seemingly random. (It's "seemingly" random because sometimes I make surreptitious choices that students are not aware of, like making sure that two students who tend to "goof off" aren't in the same group.) Students also like random groups because they never feel left out and get to work with people they wouldn't normally self-select.

If you would like to learn more about grouping methods, search for "Instructional Grouping Options" on the Internet. In the meantime, here are some ideas to get you started:

➤ Number off by the number of groups you want to end up with. For example, if you have fifteen students and you want three in each group, you will need five groups and should number off by five. You will also need to tell which group where to meet or you will have the loudest ones shouting, "Fives are here!"

➤ If you want groups of four students, get a deck of cards and pass them out randomly or fan them out and have students pick a card. Group like numbers or face cards together. If you have an uneven number, you can do one of two things. First, insert the joker(s) as a wild card. The student who draws the joker gets to pick whichever group he or she wants to work with. Second, remove some of the cards so that some groups will have only three members instead of four. If you have four groups and only fourteen students, you might remove one king and one queen so that the those groups only have three students in them.

➤ Find full-page pictures in magazines, either a very strange picture or a beautiful one. Make sure there is not too much advertising present if it is an ad. Mount the pictures on construction paper (make sure you use the same color for all of the pictures), and then cut them into two, three, or four sections. I laminate mine because I use them a lot. Make sure you have the same number of cards as students, adjusting as necessary. If I'm off by one, I have an extra card with something really strange or noticeable on it. (For me it's a squirrel's eye—don't ask!) The student who draws that gets to pick his or her group. If I'm off by more, I remove sections from some pictures. To find their group, students need to match their part of the picture with the others.

➤ If I'm grouping by opinion, for example asking students whether they agree or disagree with something, I use a technique called four corners. If students agree, they move to one corner. If they disagree, to another; if they qualify (agree under specific circumstances), to another; and if they have no clue, to the final. Then I look at the groups and make adjustments as needed. I might have three students in one corner, which is fine, but I might have ten in another, which is not.

➤ I don't know how to explain this final method. There is a mathematical way to group students so that over the course of some period of time, they will have participated in a group with all of the other members of the class. I can never figure out the formula, but I have a friend who is good at that sort of thing, and I ask her. To make this work, each student has to have (and remember) a permanent number. You call out the numbers for each of the groups, and students move to them.

There are lots and lots of other methods, but you don't want to use too many because then you will have to spend more time explaining how to get the students into groups than they will have to work in them.

Monitoring

You want group time to be focused and productive. You want students to talk about the skill you are teaching, not about the latest movie, about some other class's homework, or about random comments concerning black holes. You also want everyone to participate, not just one or two students. How do you ensure that?

You make certain that students are on task by mingling with them. Walk around the room (or between the rooms), listen in on the conversations, and make yourself available. I usually listen to the group I have my back to. That seems less intimidating to the students, and I'm likely to hear more authentic conversation. I also make sure I slowly walk by each group with an "I'm available" attitude. It's interesting to me that so many students won't raise their hand to summon me to their group, but if I'm close by, they'll grab me and ask their question. Sometimes I can stand in one spot (on the side or in the back but never in "teacher-territory" at the front and center of the room) and listen to all the conversations. But I'm not that good at multiplexing, so I keep moving. You'll develop your own monitoring ideas.

Besides making sure students are on task and answering their questions, monitoring will help you determine when to pull the groups back together. Groups will work at different rates, and you want to train them to work quickly. Sometimes I'll ask the groups to show me by raised fingers how much more time they need. If one group says none, another two say one, and a fourth says five, I'll say, "You have one more minute. Please try to finish up by then." Then I'll go to the group that is finished, review their work, and perhaps ask them to give more attention to a specific area. Make sure your minute doesn't turn into two or five. Time yourself. Otherwise you are training your students to doubt you.

Reporting

Remember that the purpose of the group work is to practice a concept with help. That means *all* members should understand it, not just one or two. Frequently, I have groups that rely on one person, the perceived "brain." The "brain," who may not even need the practice, does all of the work, and the other members, who do, skate. To prevent this, you might incorporate some accountability methods:

➤ **Note-Taking**. Require all members of the group to take notes. All of the group exercises are contained in the student book. Require students to record their thoughts there. Alternatively, sometimes I ask for these on loose-leaf paper so that they can be turned in or in a "Group Work Journal," a spiral notebook that I provide and that can only be used for group work in my class. At the beginning of the school year, the office supply stores in my area have a sale on spiral notebooks—I've seen them for as little as five cents each. I buy as many as I can and pass them out to my students. (Even if the store has limits on the number of notebooks each customer can purchase, if you say you're a teacher, they might forgo the limit.) I ask students to begin each day's group work on a new page, label the skill (Thesis Generation, for example), and date it.

As I'm walking around the room, I make sure that all of the students are writing in their books, and from time to time I collect them. Depending on the class and how much incentive they may need, I might also grade these for completion—A: extremely thorough and even more; B—thorough, well done; C—OK, minimum acceptable effort; D—lacking; F—very, very lacking.

➢ **Sharing**. I also require the groups to be prepared to share their ideas with the class as a whole. This is a critical step and so helpful to students as they hear and discuss the ideas their friends have come up with. Because there are so many different ways to form a humorous introduction, for example, I will ask several groups to share their thoughts. Not only is this helpful in understanding the skill, it also builds camaraderie as we all laugh together. I don't usually have to do too much correction at the group stage, but if I do, I make sure to do it gently and lavish praise when I can.

➢ **Presenting**. Sometimes I ask students to come to the front of the class to present their group's ideas. When I do, there's always a mad scramble to determine who will be the sacrificial lamb, and usually it boils down to the same students. But this undermines my purpose that *everyone* in the group understands and is able to explain the group's findings. Here are some ways to randomly select the presenter, and I usually announce one of these methods just before the presentation. Choose the person

    ◊   whose birthday is closest (farthest) to today
    ◊   who did/did not have rice (potatoes, vegetables, salad) for dinner last night
    ◊   who has the most (fewest) computers (televisions, radios) in the home
    ◊   who has traveled the farthest away from home
    ◊   who has visited the most number of countries
    ◊   whose grandparents live with them
    ◊   who has the most (fewest) number of people living in their home
    ◊   who has never owned a dog (cat)
    ◊   your own creative ideas

Other ways to select the presenter are to keep a list and make sure that everyone has had a chance to present by the end of some period of time, to write students' names on Popsicle sticks and draw one from a container to choose one person, and then let him or her choose the next (my students call this popcorn), or whatever. The only problem with keeping a list is that once a student has been "checked off," he or she might not be as engaged in future group work. To prevent this, you might call on a few students more than once, maybe those who aren't as fearful as others.

Speaking of fearful students, some really have a problem with talking in front of a group. It scares them witless. If you have a student like this, you might allow him or her to bring a friend for moral support. The two of them go to the front of the class, but only one talks. The other listens attentively and encourages. And by the way, you might have to teach *all* of your students how to listen attentively and encourage whoever is speaking. Try to avoid putting students in situations where they can't cope; otherwise, they will never learn to cope.

Not a Clue

At some point, you will model a skill, move students into groups, and then find out they are completely confused and off track. If this hasn't happened to you yet, it will. Even the very best of teachers will find themselves in this situation on occasion. What do you do? Stop the class, go back to the modeling, begin at the beginning, and review the steps. Your students realize they are confused, so ask them if they understand the step as you model. (A good way to do this is to ask for "thumbs": thumbs up for "I've got it"; thumbs down for "I'm still confused"; and thumbs sideways for "I'm still tentative.") Try to figure out where the disconnect occurred. It may be your teaching; it may be students' lack of attention; it may just be one of those days. When students think they are ready, resume the group work, monitor, and offer individual help where needed.

What Do Groups Do?

It's all well and good to put students into groups, but then what? What do the students *do* in their groups? You should always have a purpose for group work, and you should always be able to state it to your students: "Here's what I want you to do and why." For each of the chapters in *The Elegant Essay*, there are two sets of exercises; one to work on collaboratively in groups and another for independent practice. Beyond that, there are additional suggestions for group activities in the Lesson Plans section for each chapter.

Independent Practice

Of course the goal of your teaching is reaching the point where all of your students can perform all of the skills you teach entirely on their own. The steps we've talked about so far, mini-lecturing, modeling, and group practicing, will help students learn and will help them build those brain pathways, but the final objective is reaching the point where they can perform the skill independently. When they get home and none of their friends are around, can they still do it? The second set of exercises in each chapter provides the opportunity for independent practice, but you still need to check to see if each student "got it" or if more practice is needed. On the other hand, you don't want to get too bogged down in paperwork. Writing teachers, more than teachers of other subjects, seem to have so much paperwork to deal with already, how can they keep up and still meet the needs of their students? I have a couple of ideas.

Checking Homework

If you are teaching a class that meets once a week, you might ask students to email their homework to you a day or two before the class meets. This will give you a chance to look over what students have done well and what needs to be revisited. You might also select a few responses to share with the rest of the class and explain what is exemplary about them.

Alternatively, you might ask students to open their student books to the homework page and on some kind of a master list, check off the ones that are complete. You might do this during a pop quiz to save class time. You might check off yes or no, or you might have three categories: done with good effort, done cursorily or skimpily, and not done. If students know you are going to check, they are more apt to find time to do the work during their busy schedules.

After checking to see that the homework is done, ask students to take out a different color pen or pencil. For example, if they did the homework in pencil, they might take out a pen; if a blue pen, they might take out a green one. Tell them that as you discuss the homework as a class, you expect them to add new thoughts and clarifications to their own assignment using the new color. Then read each question and call on a student to answer it. You might randomly choose students; choose the one closest to you, and then continue in a pattern; draw a Popsicle stick with a student's name on it from a container; or choose one student, and let him or her choose the next (popcorn). Instead of asking for just one answer to a question, especially when there are choices to be made, you might call for two or three. Discuss students' answers/ideas, be affirmative, and re-teach or clarify where necessary. Once you are sure students can perform the skill you've taught, but perhaps not perfectly, you are ready to move on to the next skill.

Reviewing

After students turn in their homework, you still aren't done practicing the skill. With writing, students practice each skill in each essay they write. Because of this, review is built in, and you won't have to make up review exercises. The more students write, the more they will practice their skills. And the more they practice their skills, the more proficient they will become.

Lesson Reflection & Notes for Next Time

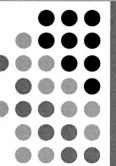

GRADING METHODS

Evaluation & Scoring Ideas

Evaluation is such a controversial issue with homeschool parents and classroom teachers, with opinions on both sides of the issue, from no grading at all to grading everything. I don't want to be dogmatic about this area, preferring to give you all the freedom you need to evaluate your own students, but I do want to offer some suggestions. Let's begin with some clarification on terminology.

Evaluation Terminology

First, I want to draw a distinction between *assessment* and *grading*.

Assessment is what you do to ensure that students understood your teaching. It helps you decide when you need to reteach or review and when to move on. Every lesson, without exception, should have some kind of assessment built into it. Further, assessment is a feedback tool. It is practice. It should not be recorded.

Grading follows assessment, sometimes by a day or two, sometimes by weeks or months. Once students have understood the skill and have had time to practice it, then they are ready to be formally evaluated. Some courses give only one opportunity for students to demonstrate their mastery of skills, such as a final exam or an Advanced Placement® test. More often though, students are given plenty of opportunity to demonstrate their mastery, like with end-of-chapter tests.

Visually, the process looks like this:

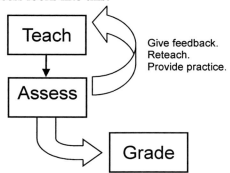

Too often, I believe, we confuse *assessment* with *grading* and move to it too quickly. On the other hand, I also believe that students do need to be graded at the appropriate time. I don't believe in no grades at all because students need the accountability. They also need a realistic understanding of their skill levels.

Perhaps you've heard other grading terminology. If so, here is how I'm using the terms:

1. Assessment—informal evaluation, formative assessment
2. Grading—formal evaluation, summative assessment

The Checklist Method

Of course, all of this begs the question: How do you grade?

I'm going to suggest two methods, one of which is in Appendix B of the student book. The other is the one I personally use, especially for Essay Boot Camp, which I teach more often than the regular course. Keep in mind that these two methods are only suggestions; you have every right to develop and use your own system. Just make sure your students understand what it is.

Checklists

Appendix B of *The Elegant Essay* contains some combination checklists and scoring guides. For example, the checklist for Chapter 2 Thesis looks like this:

- ☐ Make sure your thesis statements do not cover too much ground. Your thesis should summarize or preview your essay, not duplicate it.
- ☐ Make sure academic thesis statements are grammatically parallel.
- ☐ Remember, thesis statements may be only one sentence for these exercises.
- ☐ Check that your persuasive thesis statement presents an argument rather than states a fact.
- ☐ Check that your narrative thesis statement creates an emotion or alludes to a lesson learned.

Students are asked to create four thesis statements: a narrative, informative, persuasive, and academic. Each is worth 10 points.

When you award points, keeping with the whole idea of *assessment*, you want to grade the process rather than the product. That is, does the thesis attempt to be narrow and focused, or does it cover too much ground? Is the academic thesis grammatically parallel or not? Does the persuasive thesis contain an argument or not? You aren't looking at the quality of an argument, for example, just whether or not it's there. If the argument is there, even if it is somewhat spurious, the student gets the points. If not, he doesn't.

Since each thesis statement is worth ten points, how do you decide to award fewer? I use this method:

Grade	Descriptor	Percent	Points
A	(exceeded checklist)	90 - 100%	9 - 10
B	(met checklist)	80 - 89%	8
C	(minimum acceptable)	70 - 79%	7
D	(lacking)	60 - 69%	6
F	(not done)	50%	5

A thesis statement that met all of the checklist criteria would get all 10 points (or 9 if it was just a little off). One that was just OK would get 7, and one with deficiencies would get 6. I never award fewer than 50% credit for a student who attempts the work. I'll explain why in a minute.

Total the points for each of the four theses to arrive at the points for the exercise.

A score sheet also appears in Appendix B of the student book to keep track of the total course points.

Rubrics

When you evaluate the descriptive and persuasive essays, the situation changes a little. At this point you move from formative or informal assessment (which is basically graded on effort and attention to the checklists) to summative or formal grading. For this, a rubric works well. Keep in mind the checklist to remind students what to include in their essays. *The Elegant Essay* Grading Rubric is in Appendix B of the student book, and the Boot Camp version follows.

Note that on the rubric, the introduction is worth 10 points and asks students if it does the following:

- ☐ Captures reader's attention
- ☐ Establishes the significance of the topic
- ☐ Contains a well-formulated thesis

Since I'm now grading and considering the quality of the students' work, I would consider these three criteria and award the 10 points as follows:

Grade	Descriptor	Percent	Points
A	(amazing, outstanding, creative)	90 - 100%	9 - 10
B	(high quality)	80 - 89%	8
C	(OK, minimum acceptable)	70 - 79%	7
D	(inferior)	60 - 69%	6
F	(not done)	50%	5

I'd use the same grades, descriptors, and percentages for the body paragraphs, but since each is worth 20 points, I'd double them. So, 90% of 20 is 18, which is the grade I'd give for an A-level body paragraph. If the student only wrote two paragraphs instead of three, I'd award five points to the one not done. Again, I'll explain why in a minute.

I evaluate two versions of each student's essay—a draft and a final—and I use the same grading criteria for each. However, for the draft, instead of counting the essay as 100 points, I drop it to 90 or 95, depending on the age and experience of my students. This helps my students understand my grading criteria and improve in their areas of difficulty, and I only have to keep track of one set of standards. To determine the essay's score, add up the points for each section and record them on the Course Score Sheet.

Quizzes & Accountability

We've discussed how to grade the exercises and the essays. What's left? That depends on what you add to the course and what you want to be a part of the students' course grades. In the section on Teaching Methods, I've mentioned some ideas you might want to consider. They include

- ➤ Pop quizzes (for reading accountability)
- ➤ Open note quizzes (for engagement)
- ➤ Group work (recording groups' thoughts)

My quizzes are always worth 10 points. If the student's answer is outstanding—I couldn't ask for more—he gets 10 points. Award 9 for almost outstanding, 8 for high quality, 7 for minimally acceptable, 6 for lacking, and if the student writes something on the paper, he gets 5 points. The Course Score Sheet has a place to record quiz and accountability scores.

Determining the Grade

To calculate a student's grade, add up all the points they received, divide by the total, and multiply by 100. Then use either of these scales:

A = 90 - 100%; B = 80 - 89%; C = 70 - 79%; D = 60 - 69%

A+ = 97 - 100; A = 93 - 96; A- = 90 - 92%; B+ = 87 - 89%; B = 83 - 86%; B- = 80 - 82%
C+ = 77 - 79%; C = 73 - 76%; C- = 70 - 72%; D+ = 67 - 69%; D = 63 - 66%; D- = 60 - 62%

The Point System for Essay Boot Camp

For this slightly simplified system, the one I use especially when I'm teaching Essay Boot Camp, the persuasive essay and the quizzes are scored in the same way as in the Checklist Method. The exercises are a little different. I can't spend as much time evaluating students individually, and with the rigorous schedule, they don't usually need individual assessment anyway. I assign each exercise 10 points and award them based on the amount of effort students expended, as follows:

Grade	Descriptor	Percent	Points
A	(exceeded requirements; all attempted)	90 - 100%	9 - 10
B	(met requirements; might be skimpy)	80 - 89%	8
C	(minimum acceptable; one blank)	70 - 79%	7
D	(lacking; more than one blank)	60 - 69%	6
F	(not done)	50%	5

Since there are eight exercises (the On Your Own or independent practice/homework), the total course points works out as follows.

Exercises	80	
Quizzes	60	(Sometimes I only have time to give 4 out of the 6 quizzes and drop this score to 40 and adjust the total to 315.)
Rough Draft	95	(Persuasive Essay only)
Final Draft	100	(Persuasive Essay only)
Total	335	

The course grade is determined using the same calculation as in the Checklist Method: Add up the student's points, divide by the total (335), multiply by 100, and then use your choice of grading scales. A Course Score Sheet for the Essay Boot Camp—Point System follows in this section.

Of course, you are completely at liberty to change this scale. For example, you might choose to drop the lowest exercise score or provide feedback but not formally grade the draft. If you choose to do this, just adjust the total course points and determine new score ranges. Multiply by 90% (.9) for the A-range, 80% for the B-range, 70% for the C-range, and 60% for the D-range.

Late Work & The 50% F

I also subtract points for late work—always. Students lose one point for every day the assignment is late. If an assignment is more than five days late and the student completes it, he receives a 50 percent F (5 points). If he never does the assignment, he receives a 25 percent F (2.5 points). The reason for this has to do with math and determining an average score. If a student receives an A on one assignment and an F on another, that averages out to a C. Numerically, a 50 percent F and a 100 percent A averages out to a 75 percent C. If a student received a zero percent F, he would need to earn three A's just to offset it. I understand that life will interfere with students' performances of their responsibilities from time to time, and I will receive late assignments, but I also find that if I give students a break just once, I'm in trouble (basically because I'm a pushover).

Providing Feedback

Feedback is so important to help your students learn what they are doing well and where they need to improve. I always write uplifting comments on students' papers. Additionally, sometimes I make an audio tape for students offering further instruction. Yes, it's time-consuming, and yes, I feel very awkward talking to myself, and yes, students aren't too thrilled about this at first. But after some initial reticence, I find students love it and look forward to hearing what Mrs. Myers has to say. I try to limit these tapes to 10 - 15 minutes, and I always, *always*, begin with positive feedback. Students need to know what they are doing right. On a tape, tone of voice and excitement over small things like "cool" verbs or nice flow or interesting ideas goes a long way. To keep students accountable and to make sure I'm meeting their needs, I ask them to write a one-paragraph response to my tape. It's worth 20 points—just enough to make sure students take it seriously—and students earn all 20 points if the paragraph is completed and turned in on time. Students must do three things in their response: 1) Prove they listened to the tape by repeating something I said (and sometimes I include a special word: "Your word is 'stapler'"; 2) answer any questions I asked; and 3) give me feedback on my feedback: Did they understand my comments? Were they helpful? Do they have further questions? What else might I do as a teacher to help them with their writing? As an alternative to tapes, and because they take so much time to create, you might set up individual conferences with students.

More on Grading

If you would like more instruction on grading and evaluating, please check out my *Making the Grade* resource available from www.Cameron-Publishing.com. (Don't forget the hyphen.) Although originally designed to help homeschool parents grade and evaluate their own children, classroom teachers have also shared with me that it helped them understand their own grading process and philosophy. You might also be interested in the radio interview I did with Mike Smith on Home School Heartbeat on the same topic, available here: http://www.hslda.org/docs/hshb/82/hshbwk4.asp (or click on the link at the top of the *Making the Grade* page of http://www.cameron-publishing.com).

Elegant Essay Grading Rubric

Student: _____ Submitted on time? _____ Score _____ / 100

Introduction _____ / 10 points
- ☐ Captures reader's attention
- ☐ Establishes the significance of the topic
- ☐ Contains a well-formulated thesis

_____

_____

Body Paragraphs _____ / 60 points total (20 for each paragraph)
Circle excellent, good, fair, or poor, and then check the boxes to indicate a problem area.

Excellent, Good, Fair, Poor
- ☐ Topic/thesis connect?
- ☐ Stays on topic?
- ☐ Clear explanation?
- ☐ Clincher statement?
- ☐ Persuasive argument?

Support:
- ☐ example, personal experience, statistics, research, observation, description, anecdote/story, analogy

_____
_____
_____
_____

Excellent, Good, Fair, Poor
- ☐ Topic/thesis connect?
- ☐ Stays on topic?
- ☐ Clear explanation?
- ☐ Clincher statement?
- ☐ Persuasive argument?

Support:
- ☐ example, personal experience, statistics, research, observation, description, anecdote/story, analogy

_____
_____
_____
_____

Excellent, Good, Fair, Poor
- ☐ Topic/thesis connect?
- ☐ Stays on topic?
- ☐ Clear explanation?
- ☐ Clincher statement?
- ☐ Persuasive argument?

Support:
- ☐ example, personal experience, statistics, research, observation, description, anecdote/story, analogy

_____
_____
_____
_____

Conclusion _____ / 10 points
- ☐ Revisits thesis
- ☐ Leaves reader with something to think about
- ☐ Leaves a feeling of completeness

_____

_____

Grammar & Style _____ / 20 points
- ☐ Voice
- ☐ Mechanics
- ☐ Other Style:

The 6 + 1 Writing Traits Rubric

In the early 1980s at the Northwest Regional Educational Laboratory (NWREL), public school teachers examined thousands of student papers at all grade levels and identified six traits that were common in each. This model is now used in public and private schools all over the world. The six traits follow:

NWREL's Term	Other Terms
Ideas	Content
Organization	Structure, form
Voice	Overall expression, reader engagement, audience awareness, personality
Word Choice	Diction
Sentence Fluency	Syntax
Conventions	Mechanics, Grammar

(Note: The "+ 1" is Presentation—the paper's format or what it looks like on the page.)

The Elegant Essay has emphasized the areas NWREL calls *ideas* and *organization* and has separate rubrics for each. While I do not have permission to reprint the 6+1 rubric for these areas, I can direct you to NWREL's website where you will find them at the following links:

http://educationnorthwest.org/traits   Information on the overall process

http://educationnorthwest.org/webfm_send/773   Specific rubrics

If you find these rubrics helpful, use them. If you find them confusing, you might want to return to them another time. If you try to learn too many things at once, you will reach a point where nothing makes sense.

Name: _____   Date: _____

Class: _____   Score Sheet

Course Score Sheet for Essay Boot Camp—Point Method

Assignment	Date Turned In	Score	Possible	Comments
Exercises				
Exercise 2			10	
Exercise 4a			10	
Exercise 4b			10	
Exercise 6			10	
Exercise 8			10	
Exercise 10			10	
Exercise 13			10	
Exercise 15			10	
Essays				
Pers. Draft			95	
Pers. Final			100	
Quizzes				
Quiz #1			10	
Quiz #2			10	
Quiz #3			10	
Quiz #4			10	
Quiz #5			10	
Quiz #6			10	
Total				
			335	

Essay Boot Camp Scale:
A range: 301 - 335; B range: 268 - 300; C range: 234 - 267; D range: 201 - 233

LESSON PLANS

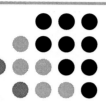

Chapter One
Overview

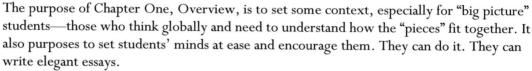

The purpose of Chapter One, Overview, is to set some context, especially for "big picture" students—those who think globally and need to understand how the "pieces" fit together. It also purposes to set students' minds at ease and encourage them. They can do it. They can write elegant essays.

Briefly review the five writing components: structure, style, content, mechanics, and overall expression. Students may have received previous instruction in style (using a variety of sentence openers, active verbs, descriptive nouns, dress-ups, and decorations). They also probably have received instruction in mechanics (grammar, spelling, and punctuation). Even though style and mechanics are not the focus of this course, students should continue practicing both as they write.

Finally, give an overview of the course through the "Taking a Journey" analogy. Students will encounter each structural element in subsequent lessons, so just introduce them at this point.

Chapter Two
Thesis Statements

<u>Big warning</u>: This is going to be the hardest section for your students to grasp. You are going to have to return to the concept of a thesis statement many, many times as you teach your students how to write essays. Don't expect too much as they encounter this strange concept for the first time. Give as much help as they need, even suggesting possible thesis statements. Yes, I mean writing their thesis statement for them. Middle school students will greatly benefit from thesis statement suggestions, but high school students will struggle as well. Even the term sounds strange to students, and you might consider calling the thesis a "mega-topic sentence" for a time and then sneak the term "thesis statement" into the conversation until it is familiar.

Pop Quiz & Entry Card Questions
Choose one or two questions.

1. What is another name for an informative essay? (expository)
2. What does a thesis statement do for readers? (keeps brains on track; establishes boundaries)
3. What is another name for a thesis statement: "_____-_____ sentence"? (mega-topic)
4. Where might you use a 3-pronged thesis statement? (in academic writing—science or history)

Lesson Specific Issues
➢ Make sure thesis statements do not cover too much ground. Students' theses should summarize or preview their essays, not duplicate them.
➢ Check academic thesis statements to be sure they are parallel. (More on this topic in the teacher's pages to Chapter 8.)
➢ Insist that thesis statements be only one sentence for these exercises.

Chapter 8, More On Thesis, returns to this topic and offers some refinements. By that time, students should be more comfortable with the whole concept.

Homework
If you choose to have students read the chapters ahead of time, students should come to class having read Chapter 2. If you feel you need to provide some kind of accountability, you might give a "pop quiz" using one or more of the questions supplied. Note: For all subsequent lessons, I'm going to assume that you have your students read the materials ahead of time.

Mini-Lecture & Modeling
Also see suggestions for lecture and modeling in the Teaching Methods section.

Ask students to take notes using the note page provided at the end of Chapter 2 as you discuss the following. Monitor students' note-taking. If a student's paper remains blank, he or she might need encouragement to stay focused or instruction in how to take notes. Provide what is needed.

Thesis Function & Essay Types (Genres)

Explain the function and purpose of a thesis statement.

One at a time, introduce the three essay genres: informative (expository), narrative (descriptive), and persuasive, as well as the academic statement. Explain their purposes, and then using the modeling exercises provided, demonstrate how to write a thesis statement for each essay type.

Demonstrate & Think Aloud

On a whiteboard, chalkboard, or easel, write the word "Informative" at the top. Explain what an informative essay does—its purpose and function.

Introduce the first topic, "friends," and write it on your board. Think out loud so that your students can follow and so that you model what they should be doing in their heads. For example you might say, "Friends. What could I write about friends? Well people need friends—everyone does. But some people are harder to love than others. How do we love the unlovable? I'm going to focus on that and think of a thesis statement that informs or explains how to love the unlovable." Write the phrase "Loving the unlovable" on your board.

Next, think out loud again: "I want to inform people that friends are very important, especially to the unlovable. How could I say that? Hmmm. How about this?" Write the thesis statement on the board as you think aloud.

At this point, your board should look something like this. (See also the student pages.)

Type: Informative

Topic	Focus/Slant/Details	Thesis Statement
Friends	Loving the unlovable	Although it may be hard, creative friends can find ways to show love to those usually unappreciated.

As you continue to model the remaining "friends" topics, try to make the modeling as interactive as you can and involve the students. The more they actively think about and come up with examples of their own, the more they will understand and remember. Suggest the next focus, "overcoming shyness," and write it on the board in the focus/slant/details column. Then ask students to help you write a thesis statement. If they look at you blankly or need more direction, suggest the second thesis statement from the modeling possibilities that follow in this section, and write it on the board. Be sure to think aloud.

Extension & Engagement

At this point, you might ask students to come up with a different thesis statement for the same focus, "overcoming shyness." Not only would this step engage students and help them work through the thesis-generating process, it would also reinforce the idea that there is no *one* right answer.

Although you want to engage the students, you also want to move your lecture and modeling along. The most important part of the lesson is student practice, so you want to leave ample time for that. If there is not enough time to model three examples of each genre, just go with two.

After you have taught and modeled how to form each of the thesis statements, return to the Developing Thesis Statements section of Chapter 2 in the student book, and review the thesis generation steps and types of thesis statements charts. Invite students to ask you questions on anything that is not clear, but remember that perfect understanding is not your goal at this step. Students need to create pathways in their own brains as they internalize the concepts you've just taught. They do this in the next step, during group work.

Practice with Help
Also see suggestions for groups in the Teaching Methods section.

<u>Group Students</u>
Divide students into groups of 2 - 4 students. Send them to different parts of the classroom/building/house, and set them to work on Exercise 1. Be sure to walk around the room(s), monitor the conversation, and provide help when needed.

If you are pressed for time, assign each group a different place to begin in the exercise. For example, Group 3 (and 7 and 11 if needed) start with number 3, continue to 4, then 1, and 2. This way when groups report to the class, at least one group will have something to say about each topic.

Something else you might try, especially if you have reluctant participants, is to require students to work independently for a short time before you divide them into groups. Some students just need a little more time to think, and this step will give it to them. Plus, they will have something to bring to the group discussion.

<u>Sharing</u>
Once students have had some group time and have completed Exercise 1, or almost completed it, call them back together and ask various groups or students to share their thoughts on one or more topics. The rest of the class should be adding new ideas to their papers based on what they hear. I ask students to do this in a different color pen or pencil so that I can monitor their engagement.

If you feel your class's examples lack in some way or another, choose some examples from the One Class's Answers to share.

On Your Own
Also see teaching suggestions for homework / independent practice in the Teaching Methods section.

Assign Exercise 2 as homework. Homework or independent practice should provide students the opportunity to practice what they have learned as well as give you feedback on what they have absorbed and what may need to review further. You will need to develop a plan to address the specific issues that you see after reviewing the homework.

It's always a good idea to share exemplary answers to the Exercises. If students share quality thesis statements, praise them profusely. If not, select some from the One Class's Answers to Exercise 2 to share.

Modeling

Thesis Statements

Directions: Using a whiteboard or tablet, write down the essay type and topic, and then brainstorm with your students to develop a thesis statement for each slant or set of details.

Essay Type	Topic	Focus/Slant/ Details	Possible Thesis
Expository (Informative)	Friends	Loving the unlovable	Although it may be hard, creative friends can find ways to show love to those usually unappreciated.
		Overcoming shyness	With a little effort, shy people can learn to be comfortable around groups.
		Bible verses	The Bible says quite a bit about friends, especially in the book of Proverbs.
Narrative (Descriptive)	Holidays	Nostalgic	Paper ornaments, burning candles, and bustling kitchens highlighted the Christmas of Victorian times.
		Time for family	Battling traffic and crowds, families travel many miles to join each other in a festive Christmas celebration.
		Stressful/ hectic	One year our family decided to spend the Christmas holiday in Hawaii; unfortunately, when we reached the airport, half the city joined us.
Persuasive	Television	Harmful	Unlimited television viewing can harm children.
		Wasteful	Watching too much television steals valuable time from other pursuits.
		Enjoyable	At the end of a weary day, television can refresh the mind and body.
Academic/ Informative	Career	Fulfilling Secure Profitable	Upon graduation, college students look for fulfilling, secure, and profitable careers.
Academic/ Persuasive	Smoking	Health Cost Image	Cigarette smoking damages a person's health, consumes a family's finances, and presents a poor image.

Exercise 1

Develop thesis statements for the following topics. Make sure one example uses an academic thesis.

1. **Courage**

   Persuasive: With knowledge, time, and hard work, courageous people can work together to overcome evil.

   Informative: When courage is mentioned in advertising, it is effective in getting boys to enlist in the military.

   Academic: Courage can help one acquire the ability to help others, complete a goal, and set an example.

   Informative: Soldiers at Normandy braved tremendous machine gun and mortar fire while they were advancing towards the German positions.

   Informative: Since a policeman's work is so hazardous, he must display courage.

   Persuasive: Courage gives people the willingness to help others in need.

   Informative: Courage, correctly defined, is fear motivated to do the right thing.

   Informative: The fact that most people would rather face death than speak in public illustrates how vital courage is to public speaking.

2. **A gift**

   Descriptive: The present on the table was addressed to me, but its origins were tightly wrapped in secrecy.

   Informative: While a gift given at a good time can be a wonderful thing, a gift given at a bad time can be fatal or destructive.

   Persuasive: Giving a gift to someone not only gives you pleasure but also allows the receiver to experience happiness.

   Persuasive: A guest in someone's home should always bring the hostess a gift because it shows good manners.

   Persuasive: A husband should always remember to give his wife an anniversary gift, unless he is prepared to sleep on the couch.

   Informative: A gift can be a fun and happy thing for the person who receives it.

   Academic: Gift-giving expresses affection, care, and admiration towards another.

3. **Women in the military**

   Informative: Women in the Navy are restricted from serving in submarines because of confined spaces with male submariners.

   Informative: Women who serve in the military help their country greatly.

   Informative: The Navy does not allow women to be Seals because women are weaker than men and could endanger their own health.

   Persuasive: Because the Bible says it's a man's duty, women should not be allowed to serve in the military.

   Persuasive: With the possible exception of combat, women make very effective soldiers.

   Persuasive: Although women are unmatched in maternal, protective instincts, they are better off protecting their children rather than their nation.

4. **Education**

   Academic: Independent study at both the high school and college level builds self-motivation, encourages deeper study, and frees the student from repetitive classes.

   Academic: A good education consists of three phases: grade school, high school, and college.

   Informative: Parents strengthen their child's character when they spend time educating him.

   Academic: Homeschooling is a wise form of education because it encourages strong family ties, academic excellence, and good time management skills.

   Persuasive: More Christian parents should teach their children at home in order to model Christian values, give them a practical education, and foster strong family ties.

   Informative: A good education opens opportunities for one in life.

   Informative: Being home-educated gives students more flexibility and time for extracurricular activities.

   Informative: If people get a good education, their chances for financial security usually increase.

Exercise 2

Develop thesis statements for the following topics. Make sure one example uses an academic thesis.

1. **Socialism**

   Persuasive: Socialism does not create better health care for the less fortunate; in fact, it divests hospitals of supplies and equipment.

   Persuasive: Socialism will never succeed because of its reliance on the goodness of man.

   Informative: Socialism is a government-run society where control is in the hands of the government and people have little power over their lives.

   Persuasive: The Union of the Soviet Socialist Republics collapsed because of its flawed foreign and domestic policies.

   Persuasive: Socialism is an unwise economic system because it gives the government too much control.

   Academic: Socialism maintains its grasp on its citizens by restricting their freedoms to go where they wish, say what they think, and worship anything but the state.

2. **A favorite teacher**

   Descriptive: Whoever thought school was boring never met my teacher; pencil eagerly poised, I waited on her every word.

   Descriptive: My favorite teacher may be strict, but with her friendly smile she's always willing to help.

   Informative: My piano teacher is my favorite educator because she is encouraging and well-qualified.

   Informative: A good teacher inspires good learning.

   Academic: I met my favorite teacher in third grade; he influenced me spiritually, encouraged me emotionally, and inspired me musically.

   Persuasive: Picking a favorite teacher could limit your opportunity to learn, especially if you are not willing to give another teacher a chance.

   Academic: A good teacher is easy to understand, fun to learn from, and willing to answer questions with clarity.

3. **College**

   Academic: A college education can help in later life, benefit financially, and lend a feeling of personal accomplishment.

   Informative: College helps one get a good job with financial rewards and personal fulfillment.

   Persuasive: Most Americans think that to be smart you have to go to college; this mindset is shortsighted and ignorant.

   Descriptive: The mere thought of college—the new people I will meet and the things I will learn—makes me want to pack up and start right now.

   Persuasive: Before people graduate from high school, it's important that they know whether they want to attend college.

   Academic: To obtain a degree, students may enroll in a traditional college, take classes over the Internet, or sit for exams after studying on their own.

4. **Ministry or community service**

   Informative: Community service does more than fill blanks on college applications; it provides teens with a way to help others.

   Informative: Not only is serving in a community important, it helps others and lets them know someone cares.

   Persuasive: People should participate in ministry because God commands us to serve others, and when we obey Him, He gives us joy.

   Informative: Short-term mission trips to Mexico are designed to help the local populations with physical and spiritual needs.

Lesson Reflection & Notes for Next Time

Chapter Three
Essay Organization

This chapter introduces students to a very simple paragraph structure, to the difference between *showing* and *telling*, as well as to eight ways they might support the thesis statements they created in Chapter 2. Depending on the age and experience of your students, you should plan on spending twice as long on this chapter as you do on others, first introducing the simple paragraph structure and demonstrating the difference between *showing* and *telling,* and then moving on to the eight support ideas. (These three areas are each addressed separately in these teacher materials.) You can stop your lesson where convenient, and when you pick up again, be sure to spend a few minutes reviewing.

Pop Quiz & Entry Card Questions

1. In terms of support, what is the difference between an example and personal experience? (Example pertains to someone else; personal experience must be one's own.)
2. List and describe three of the eight kinds of evidence. (example, personal experience, statistics, research, observation, description, anecdote, analogy)
3. What does SEE stand for? (Statement, Example, Explanation)
4. What is the difference between *showing* and *telling*? (Showing creates an image in a reader's brain; telling just states facts.)

Lesson Specific Issues

➢ The simple structure is a means to teach students how to organize a paragraph. Students should understand the process but should not write every paragraph using this formula—otherwise their writing will begin to sound stilted, not to mention boring.

➢ Students might become confused if you introduce all of the evidence and support techniques at once. You might spread them out over some period of time.

➢ Students will like one kind of evidence more than another and might overuse one technique at the expense of others. Encourage (require) them to use a variety.

Mini-Lecture & Modeling of Simple Structure (SEE)
Also see suggestions for lecture and modeling in the Teaching Methods section.

Ask students to take notes using the note page provided at the end of Chapter 3 as you discuss the following. Monitor students' note-taking. If a student's paper remains blank, he or she might need encouragement to stay focused or instruction in how to take notes. Provide what is needed.

Demonstrate the simple structure on a previously-written paragraph or use Modeling Exercise #1 in the Student Notes section. With four different colors of ink, underline the topic and clincher sentences (red), the statement (blue), the first example or explanation (green), and the second example or explanation (black). Repeat for the second SEE. The color-coding will help students differentiate between the four parts of the paragraph's structure.

(**Topic—Red**) Peer pressure sometimes prevents people from listening to their consciences. (**Statement—Blue**) A young person might hear companions spreading false rumors or gossiping about a close friend. (**First Example—Green**) No one wants to go against the crowd. (**Second Example—Black**) Speaking out, even graciously, takes fortitude. (**Statement—Blue**) Alternatively, people might face the temptation to set aside their standards. (**First Example—Green**) If friends want to watch a movie filled with violence or inappropriate content, the person faces a quandary. (**Second Example—Black**) Should he go along with the group and watch or affirm his standards and leave? (**Clincher—Red**) By exhibiting courage, people stay true to their beliefs and principles.

Now direct students to the second modeling paragraph, and ask them to identify and color code each sentence:

(**Topic—Red**) When parents give gifts to their children, they send a special message of love. (**Statement—Blue**) They say they care in a very real way. (**First Example—Green**) For example, if a child wants a computer for Christmas, parents might work hard to provide it. (**Second Example—Black**) They might even sacrifice receiving their own gifts to buy it. (**Clincher—Red**) Their actions communicate their love.

The objective of the above exercise is to demonstrate the simplest or most basic essay **structure**—that in addition to topic and clincher statements, which students should already be able to write, body paragraphs need to include some kind of support and discussion, in this case, a SEE. However, you should also point out that in terms of **content**, these paragraphs are extremely lacking. First they rely on hypothetical examples—I call these if-land or might-land—the weakest of all support. Second, they are completely *telling*. Emphasize that while just barely OK, this kind of body paragraph should be written only under the most pressing of emergency situations. For grade-motivated students, you might say that it will never earn more than a C. Higher scoring and better paragraphs will *show* in addition to *tell*.

Mini-Lecture & Modeling Showing vs. Telling

Showing is always superior to telling when used as support for essays because it involves the audience and instead of telling them what to think, it allows them to experience the action or evidence and make up their own minds. Use the three examples in the Showing vs. Telling section of Chapter 3 to model the difference between the two. Then put students into pairs and ask them to rewrite statements such as the following:

➢ Dad is very funny.
➢ Mom sometimes forgets things.
➢ The cat was afraid of Tora, the very brave dog.
➢ [Students' favorite sport] is fun.

Students usually enjoy this activity. If they have trouble, ask them questions: Why is basketball fun? What is your favorite part? Can you picture yourself having fun with basketball? Do you remember a specific situation? What did/does that look like? If they still have trouble, you might ask them to act out or pantomime the situation before writing about it.

Mini-Lecture & Modeling the Eight Kinds of Support

To introduce and demonstrate the difference between a telling paragraph and a showing paragraph, refer to the simple structure of the gift-giving paragraph on the previous page:

> **(Topic—Red)** When parents give gifts to their children, they send a special message of love. **(Statement—Blue)** They say they care in a very real way. **(First Example—Green)** For example, if a child wants a computer for Christmas, parents might work hard to provide it. **(Second Example—Black)** They might even sacrifice receiving their own gifts to buy it. **(Clincher—Red)** Their actions communicate their love.

Although this paragraph is OK (just barely), it could definitely be improved. Introduce personal experience as a type of support (see student book) and model how it could be used to improve the paragraph. Big cautionary note: The student book offers the admonition that their personal experience must be true, not something that they make up. Therefore, unless this really happened to you, you should make sure students understand it is a model from the teacher's pages.

> **(Topic—Red)** When parents give gifts to their children, they send a special message of love. **(Statement—Blue)** They say that they care in a very real way. **(First Example—Green)** One Christmas I wanted a computer with a special game station. I told my parents that I didn't want anything else, just the computer. My mom tried to explain to me that computers cost a lot of money and they just couldn't afford to buy me one. I insisted. In fact, I pouted. It was the computer or nothing. Christmas day arrived and I rushed to the tree. There it was! I was thrilled and played on it all day. **(Second Example—Black)** Later, I asked my mom what present she received for Christmas. She said she didn't really need anything, and she and dad might go shopping during the after-Christmas sales. That's when I realized that both Mom and Dad had sacrificed their own gifts so that they could buy my computer. I felt guilty, but I also realized how much my mom and dad loved me. **(Clincher—Red)** Their actions communicated their love.

It will take too much time to model a paragraph for each of the seven remaining support ideas, and usually it is not necessary. Instead, look at and discuss each of the ideas under the modeling suggestions and return to the examples in the student book as necessary.

Modeling

Body Paragraphs

<u>Essay Type</u>: Informative
<u>Support</u>: Personal Experience
<u>Thesis</u>: Gift-giving expresses affection and admiration.
<u>Body</u>: See above
<u>Other ideas</u>:

➢ **Example**: An example relates someone else's experience. Students could write about a time when their friend or someone in their family gave or received a meaning-filled gift.

> **Statistics**: A bit of Internet research might reveal the amount of money people spend on gifts, perhaps at Christmas time.

> **Observation**: Observations show reasoning and often include the words *might* or *could*. Students might observe that a small gift could accompany an apology and express regret.

> **Research**: Research in terms of expert testimony might be a little difficult for this topic. However, students might be able to research the origin of gift-giving and compare its original purpose to today's use.

> **Description**: In the example above, students might describe the computer or alternatively, the anticipation of rushing to the tree, tearing off the present's wrappings, and setting up the new station.

> **Anecdote/Story**: Although the above example relates personal experience, it also uses a story. Students could relate stories that happened to them or to others. For a Christmas story, students might retell the legend of the little drummer boy or St. Nicholas.

> **Analogy**: Students might compare gifts to kind words. Both express love and affection. Your student might experience difficulty with analogies, comparing something known to explain something else. If so, return to them another time.

Practice with Help
Also see suggestions for groups in the Teaching Methods section.

Group Students
The way you approach this part of your lesson will depend on the number of students you are teaching. Ideally, students should have exposure to each technique.

> If you are teaching one student, that might not be possible. For him or her, do the practice exercises together (with him or her doing most of the work) on four different techniques using Exercise 3a and 3b, and then talk about ideas for the others but don't require more practice paragraphs. For the independent work (homework), ask your student to practice the remaining four techniques.

> If you have a larger class or co-op, use a grouping technique and divide students into pairs (or trios, but pairs work better) and assign each group a support technique. If you want groups to do statistics and research, you might allow students to make things up *for this exercise only*, or you might plan ahead, do the research, and provide it for the students.

Write Paragraphs
Students should gather ideas and write their paragraphs in their student book, but they also need to display them to visually share them with the rest of the class. Supply students with a large piece of chart paper and a marker, and ask them to write the final version of their paragraph on it. Their lettering should be large enough for the class to read, but not so giant that they need several pieces of paper.

Give students a few minutes to get started, and then as students are writing, walk around the class, monitor progress, and give help where needed. Be encouraging. As you see students completing their work, give a two-minute warning, draw the class back together, and give instructions for the next part of the group work.

<u>Share Paragraphs</u>

Since one of the objectives of the Practice with Help step is to engage students' brains and help them to internalize the concept you are teaching, it's always a good idea to solicit their thoughts on their peers' efforts. If students have difficulty expressing themselves in an encouraging way, you might have to explicitly teach them how to do this.

Tape the paragraphs to the walls of the room along with blank comment sheets next to each. Start each group on the paragraph to the right of theirs. Give students a few minutes to read the paragraph and write comments about its effectiveness on the sheets. Don't give students too much time at each paragraph, otherwise subsequent groups might not have anything to add. When you call "switch," groups should rotate in a clockwise motion; that way at the end of the time they will end up at their own paragraph and will be able to read the students' comments about their work. Here are some ideas students should look for and comment on:

➢ Is the paragraph understandable? Good topic, clincher, and flow?
➢ Does the evidence support the assertion?
➢ What is done well?
➢ What might be improved?

In addition to monitoring the students, you should also be reading the paragraphs and comments. At the end of the activity, call students back together, address problem areas, and highlight exemplary efforts.

Ideally, at the end of your Practice with Help session (or sessions if you teach the lessons over multiple days or weeks as recommended), students will have had exposure to all eight kinds of evidence and will be prepared to try them out in their own writing.

To wrap up the Practice with Help session, share and discuss the One Class's Answers sample response to Exercise 3 on the next page.

On Your Own

Also see teaching suggestions for homework / independent practice in the Teaching Methods section.

Assign Exercise 4 as homework and assess student progress. Develop a plan to address difficulties or reteach problem areas. It's always a good idea to share exemplary answers to the exercises, and if students submit their responses to you via email, you can select one or two for consideration. Never select student work to serve as a poor example. Instead, make up your own example. If you don't receive anything you would like to share, use the sample in One Class's Answers to Exercise 4 on the next page.

Exercise 3

Answers will vary for these exercises. Students may use thesis statements they've already developed or come up with new ones.

<u>Thesis</u>: Courageous people are often made, not born.

<u>Type of Support</u>: Example

People never know when they might be called upon to act courageously. They may encounter unforeseen situations and need to make quick decisions. This was the case in 1982 when an Air Florida plane crashed and quickly sank near the 14th Street Bridge in Washington, D.C. Most of the passengers died in the icy Potomac River, but five were rescued by courageous people, including Arland D. Williams, a fellow passenger. When helicopters dropped lifelines to the stranded people clinging to the plane's tailpiece, twice Williams caught the line and passed it to another. His courage saved others but sadly not himself. He drowned before helicopters could return for him. That morning Williams was just a businessman taking a trip. By evening, he was a hero whose courageous actions earned him a place in the hearts of those who had watched the entire ordeal on their televisions. The unfortunate crash had called for a courageous act, and an ordinary bank examiner performed it.

Exercise 4

Answers will vary for these exercises. Students may use thesis statements they've already developed.

<u>Thesis</u>: Community service does more than fill blanks on college applications; it provides teens with a way to help others.

<u>Type of Support</u>: Personal Experience

Even though teens may volunteer for the wrong reasons, they can experience a change of heart and gain a sense of fulfillment. This happened to me. I will admit that when I was asked to serve Thanksgiving dinner to the homeless, I wasn't too excited. Thanksgiving was a family holiday, and I didn't want to spend it with scruffy people I didn't even know. Then I met Mary. Abandoned by her husband, Mary tried to support her two children, but ran out of paycheck before she ran out of month. Shyly, she thanked me for serving what was probably the only meal she had that day. I felt ashamed of my attitude and determined to look at homeless people with new eyes. Since then I've volunteered to help serve the homeless every Thanksgiving. Not only that, but my family has joined me. My brother and my parents have all experienced the joy of serving others.

Chapter Four
Transitions

This is a pretty straightforward chapter, and students catch on to it pretty quickly. The *bridge* transition is taught in the student pages but not practiced. Students will return to bridge transitions in Chapter 7 once they start writing multiple paragraphs.

Pop Quiz & Entry Card Questions

1. List and define the three kinds of transitions (yellow line—to continue with a thought; road signs—to change or move to a new thought; bridge—to hook paragraphs together).

Lesson Specific Issues

➢ A *Synonym Finder* or thesaurus might help to find words that reflect or replace another similar word for variety. Sometimes students overuse certain words.

➢ For more transition ideas, I highly recommend Victor Pellegrino's *Transitional Words and Expressions*.

➢ When illustrating a point with a Bible verse (or other quotation), make sure students make a transition to it. They might include a phrase such as "As [Bible verse] illustrates…" or "In [Bible verse] God says…" Watch for this, especially in the Spurgeon excerpts.

➢ Period goes inside quotation marks.
  <u>Correct</u>: He said, "Excuse me." <u>Incorrect</u>: He said, "Excuse me".

➢ Correct Bible verse citation: "Jesus wept" (John 11:35). <u>Note</u> no period after *wept*. It goes after the right parenthesis.

➢ Encourage students to combine sentences in the exercises.

Mini-Lecture & Modeling

<u>Teaching Transitions</u>

To begin your mini-lecture and visually demonstrate how important transitions are, enlist the help of a student. Tell your class the student is the reader and you are the writer. The two of you begin walking together. You understand each other and all is well. Then you make a turn while the student keeps walking forward. What happened? Someone missed a transition. Maybe it was too obscure, or maybe it was missing. In any case, this is exactly what happens with readers when transitions are lacking—the reader and writer end up miles apart.

Delineate the difference between yellow line and road sign transitions and the purpose of each. Share some sentences that use yellow line transitions (These are listed on the note page.):

➢ **Pronouns**: Last Saturday afternoon, Tom went to the movies. He saw a terrific show.

➢ **Repeated words**: As to special effects, they were incredible, and Tom immediately came home to research how they were done.

➢ **Synonyms**: Surprisingly, his investigation revealed that the movie studio had found a way to create a new interface between computer generated graphics and film.

> ➢ **Repeated thoughts**: Learning about how the special effects were created made Tom appreciate the movie even more.

Next, ask students to review the road sign transitions in their book, and call on some to make up sentences using the transitional words. The purpose of this activity is to introduce your students to a variety of transitional words and allow them to hear the words used orally. To make the activity a little more interesting, you might award a small prize (a piece of candy, a weird sticker) to the student who uses the transitional word correctly while coming up with the funniest or most ridiculous or most profound sentence.

Spend most of your time on yellow line and road sign transitions, but be sure to introduce bridges as well. Tell students bridges are used to link the thoughts of paragraphs together and will be revisited in a subsequent lesson.

<u>Using Transitions</u>

Once your students understand the kinds of transitions and have had some practice using them, move on to the modeling. Write the eight modeling sentences on the left side of your whiteboard or chart paper, or direct students to Appendix A in their books. An overhead or PowerPoint slide will not work as well because students should be able to see the original sentences as you write your paragraph.

Draw a line down the middle of the whiteboard (or use a different color marker), and write a paragraph using the listed sentences. Cross them off after you use them. It's always a good idea to think aloud as you make your choices: "Let's see . . . What do I think would be a good idea to start my paragraph with?. . . What should follow? . . . Have I linked the sentences together? Do they make sense and flow? . . . If not, what changes do I have to make?"

As you can see with the resulting paragraph, not every sentence requires a transition, for example, the final sentence. However, it maintains the flow of ideas because it is perfectly reasonable to go somewhere for additional information. The only sentence that uses a road sign is the one that begins, "In fact." The rest are yellow line—repeated words, synonyms, and ideas.

Practice with Help
Also see suggestions for groups in the Teaching Methods section.

Group students using a previously discussed method into groups of three. Although not entirely necessary, one fun way to approach the practice exercise and support kinesthetic learners is to make copies for each group of the Sentence Strips for Exercise 5 found on page 49 of these notes, and cut them apart. Give each group a set, a glue stick, and a piece of construction paper.

Groups should manipulate sentence strips, feeling free to combine sentences if they want. When they've reached a consensus about order, they should glue sentence strips to the construction paper, and edit them so that most contain yellow line or road sign transitions and so that all make sense and flow. The finished product should be copied into students' books.

When most have finished, call the class back together and ask groups to share. Since this is an easy, non-threatening sharing, you might call on your more reticent students. Make them come to the front of the room and read their paragraphs. You will be helping them expand their comfort zone while practicing transitions. Call on several groups, and discuss the choices that each one made.

If desired, you might share samples from One Class's Answers to Exercise 5 on page 48.

Modeling

Transitions

Put the following sentences in order; then add transitional words or phrases between sentences to form a complete paragraph. Do not change the substance of any sentence, although you may change the wording or structure.

1. One thousand students have taken advantage of this opportunity since it began in 1985.
2. "I've heard a lot of great feedback from the program. So many students are really glad they went," commented Dr. Thomas Johnson, the study's organizer.
3. For more information contact the university at 999-9999 or www.university.com.
4. Students can participate in other international study programs, including Brazil, Mexico, and Spain.
5. The London staff focuses on art, history, and humanities.
6. The course is challenging.
7. Students at the local university can earn the opportunity to study in London or Paris.
8. Time for field trips is included.

This semester, students at the local university can earn the opportunity to study in London or Paris. In fact, one thousand students have taken advantage of this opportunity since it began in 1985. "I've heard a lot of great feedback from the program. So many students are really glad they went," commented Dr. Thomas Johnson, the study's organizer. The London staff focuses on art, history, and humanities, but students can also participate in other international study programs, including Brazil, Mexico, and Spain. The course is challenging; nevertheless, time for field trips is included. For more information, contact the university at 999-9999 or www.university.com.

On Your Own
Also see teaching suggestions for homework / independent practice in the Teaching Methods section.

Assign Exercise 6 as homework and assess student progress. Develop a plan to address difficulties or reteach problem areas. It's always a good idea to share exemplary answers to the exercises, and if students submit their responses to you via email, you can select one or two for consideration. Never select student work to serve as a poor example. Instead, make up your own example. If you don't receive anything you would like to share, use the sample in One Class's Answers to Exercise 6 on pages 48 - 49.

Cool Kite Competition

At the second annual Cool Kite Competition next week, kites will soar over our town. The public may participate in the competition or just bring a picnic lunch and watch. The event is free. Competitors will be divided into two groups: twelve and over, and under twelve. Winners will receive gift certificates to Cool Kites. Cool Kites was organized to attract the public to visit the newly refurbished reservoirs. Last year's event drew 300 participants. (Amber Myers)

Kites will soar over our town in the second annual Cool Kite Competition next month. This event was organized to attract the public to the newly refurbished reservoirs. Last year the Cool Kite Competition drew 300 participants. This year the public is once again invited to fly a kite or watch demonstrations. Two age groups of kite flyers will compete: twelve and over, and under twelve, with all winners receiving gift certificates to Cool Kites. The event is free, so bring a picnic lunch and join the fun! (Brianna Swanson)

Spectacular kites will soar over our town next month during the second annual Cool Kite Competition. Cool Kite Competition was organized to attract the public to the newly refurbished reservoirs. There will be two competition groups: twelve and over, and under twelve. Last year, 300 people participated in this event. The winners will receive gift certificates to Cool Kites. The public is invited to fly a kite or watch demonstrations, and participants may bring a picnic. (Emily Turner)

Living for Christ

We live in near fellowship with the Lord Jesus and need to seek to tread in His footsteps. By doing so, we will grow like Him. Just like the soldier fights for his captain and shares in his captain's victory, the believer needs to contend for Christ and partake of his Master's triumph. As it says in Philippians 1:21, "For me to live is Christ." Christ is the object of our lives. (Amber Myers)

The soldier fights for his captain and shares in his captain's victory. In the same way the believer contends for Christ and partakes of his Master's triumph; as the Bible says, "For me to live is Christ" (Philippians 1:21). Christ is the object of our life. We grow like Him when we live in near fellowship with the Lord Jesus and when we seek to tread in His footsteps. (Bruce Cork)

Philippians 1:21 says, "For me to live is Christ." As the soldier fights for his captain and

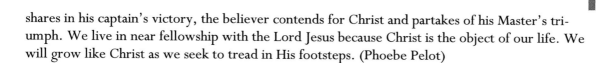

shares in his captain's victory, the believer contends for Christ and partakes of his Master's triumph. We live in near fellowship with the Lord Jesus because Christ is the object of our life. We will grow like Christ as we seek to tread in His footsteps. (Phoebe Pelot)

Sentence Strips for Exercise 5
Copy and cut out the following sentences. You will need one set for each group.

1. There will be two kite competition groups: twelve and over, and under twelve.

2. Participants may bring a picnic.

3. The public is invited to fly a kite or watch demonstrations.

4. The event is free.

5. Last year's event drew 300 participants.

6. Cool Kite Competition was organized to attract the public to the newly refurbished reservoirs.

7. Winners will receive gift certificates to Cool Kites.

8. Kites will soar over our town in the second annual Cool Kite Competition next month.

Lesson Reflection & Notes for Next Time

Chapter Five
Introductions

● ● ● ● ● ● ● ● ● ● ● ● ● ● ●

Face it, most essays are rather dull. Not that they have to be or should be, but they are. Not the ones that your students write or mine either, but the majority of essays written in schools across the country are inordinately blasé. In fact, I do believe that some teachers encourage lifeless essays, including many (but thankfully not all) science and history teachers. What is a creative student to do?

For many students, especially those with an excess of creative juices, introductions are their favorite part of essay-writing. It's the first place that they can wax eloquent with impunity. These creative souls eventually develop their own personal writing voice (or writing personality), but that takes time and effort. Introductions are easier. Encourage your students to have fun with this chapter. Reward and praise their efforts.

Pop Quizzes and Entry Cards
1. What is a funnel? (an introduction that gives background and introduces the thesis)
2. There are seven different kinds of introductory techniques. Name three. (funnel, question, benefit, funny or startling statement, quotation, dialogue, story)
3. What is the main purpose of an introduction? (Hook the reader's attention—make him or her want to keep reading.)
4. What is a dramatic opening? (an opening that is particularly engaging, usually a story with action, that precedes the "real" introduction)
5. What is one problem with many introductions? (omitting them, starting too early, dull)

Lesson Specific Issues
➤ Introductions should compose an entire paragraph, not just one sentence. Many of my students' introductions are too brief.
➤ Encourage students to rewrite the entire introductory paragraph in the exercises rather than just to tack on another sentence, such as a question, startling statement, or quotation. They should also feel at liberty to change some of the words, especially the verbs.
➤ When adding creative details, be careful students do not stray too far away from the original topic.
➤ Be sure dialogue or a startling statement connects with the rest of the introduction.
➤ Disallow statements like, "By reading this essay…" or "I intend to show…" or "By way of introduction. . . ."
➤ Completely disallow any "I" statements in the introduction: "I think," "I believe," others.
➤ Require your student to try *all* of the introductory techniques. You might have to help with content, suggesting a quotation or Bible verse, for example.
➤ My favorite source for quotations is www.ThinkExist.com. Others include the following Web sites: www.quotationspage.com, www.quoteland.com, and www.brainyquote.com.
➤ Make sure the introduction makes sense and uses good transitions.

Mini-Lecture & Modeling

You're not going to have to introduce your students to introductions. No doubt they are completely familiar with them and have struggled with them in other assignments, from book reports to research reports. In fact, you might hear an audible groan as you introduce today's topic. To sever this line of thought, emphasize that today's lesson will draw on students' creativity.

You might begin by asking how many students would rather write a story in place of an essay or how may prefer creative writing to expository (non-fiction) writing. You probably will have a few. Reassure them that today the rest of the class will need their talents. No, they can't write an entire story with a beginning, middle, climax, and end (which, actually, I've had students try to do), but they can be creative. This should come as a welcome relief after the highly technical chapters on thesis generation, body paragraphs with evidence, and transitions.

It's important to model each of the introductory techniques on the same topic to show students that the topic does not necessarily limit the kind of introductory technique available. First, read the funnel introduction in the modeling techniques below. Put it up on an overhead, PowerPoint slide, or big piece of chart paper, or write it on your whiteboard. Discuss it with your students. Does it make them want to continue reading? Is it compelling? What does it lack? I'm hoping someone will say that it is lifeless. Although there's nothing wrong with the content, the presentation leaves something to be desired. Tell your students you will be looking for ways to make this introduction more appealing.

Student Book

Direct students to the seven types of introductions in their book. You might call on individual students (See possible methods discussed elsewhere.) to read each of the examples. After discussing the examples in the student pages, return to the model. Ask students questions, interact with them to come up with introductory options for the model, and write notes about them on the board. If your students' ideas are better than mine and they generate more creative ideas, excellent! This is what you want—creativity.

Model Examples

After discussing students' ideas, you might read aloud each of the intro techniques in the modeling that follows. If you have students who have difficulty processing information audibly, you will also have to show the model visually. Overheads and PowerPoint slides are the easiest. You might also direct them to the models in Appendix A of their books, but make sure students do not read the model until after you have solicited their ideas. (You might ask students to cover the page with a piece of scrap paper and reveal only one technique at a time.)

Notes on the Models

> **Question.** Note that the question model actually contains three questions. This is fine; however, if students decide to ask more than one question, they should strive for three. Two is too few, and the effect lessens with more than three.

> **Benefit.** The benefit in this example is that God is glorified. Students might also infer that another benefit is being a good witness for the Lord so we can share Christ with others.

> **Humor.** While this particular example is not exactly funny, it does startle. Two good ways to write a startling statement are to take a worn-out cliché and twist it or

to take a common saying (as in this case) and redirect it. Note also that the same student wrote the second and fourth examples, and they sound a bit similar. This is fine as long as each demonstrates the specific technique.

- ➤ **Quotation.** "Just say no" was a popular phrase at the time this introduction was written. It may not be as familiar to your students.
- ➤ **Dialogue.** Conversation does not have to be authentic as long as it sounds made up, like this example.
- ➤ **Story.** The key to the story is description and imagery (appeal to the senses). It is not a full-blown, multi-page actual story (which some students really, really want to write).

Practice with Help
Also see suggestions for groups in the Teaching Methods section.

Groups of three or four work well for this exercise. Depending on the size of your class, assign each group a specific technique to try. If you have a class of at least 18, assign all of the techniques, doubling up where needed. If you have fewer, assign three or four of the techniques, one per group.

First Sharing
Give students a few minutes to come up with an introductory idea for their particular technique for Exercise 7. While the whole group collaborates on the ideas, students should write the group's introduction in their student book. This is extremely important because it ensures that everyone is engaged and that all students will have examples to refer to when they do the independent practice on their own.

When students have had time to work out their ideas (perhaps give a two-minute warning), call everyone back together and ask groups to share. Since this is a low-key, non-threatening kind of sharing, you might call on your more reticent students, but any sharing method is fine. Ask students to read their introductions aloud to the class, comment on them, and lavish praise and encouragement where you can. Direct the class to write notes in the spaces provided in Exercise 7 so that they will remember techniques they like. In my experience, even the students who don't like to learn audibly have no difficulty with listening to groups report orally. That's because the introductions are *interesting* and hook attention, which is the goal.

Second Sharing
After the first sharing, assign the remainder of the techniques, or if all were demonstrated the first time, allow students to pick a new one they would like to try. Strive for variety though. It's not that interesting to listen to six question introductions in a row. Direct students to write their group's introduction in their student books, and then call on students to share as above.

On Your Own
Assign students Exercise 8 to do on their own. They should complete the entire exercise and have examples for each introductory technique. When you discuss these exercises, draw on One Class's Answers as needed for models.

Introductory Techniques

1. Funnel

A Christian's speech must glorify the Lord at all times. Grace should season each sentence. Sometimes, however, Christians face tough situations. Sometimes they need to warn or confront. Sometimes they need to turn conversations around. Above all, Christians need to use their time wisely and not over-commit themselves. They must learn to say "no" graciously.

2. Ask a question.

Have you ever wanted to remove your foot from your mouth? Do you wish you could speak more kindly to others? Does your speech glorify God and show His love? As Christians, we are called to lead a life pleasing to God. This includes our speech. We must learn to speak courteously, exhort each other kindly, and say "no" graciously. (Samara Meahan)

3. Show a benefit to be gained.

Christians have many opportunities to be godly examples to unbelievers. By taking heed of how we talk, we, as Christians, can control the conversations we are in. It is always important to be gracious no matter what. If we are talking to someone and they are not glorifying God, it is our responsibility to turn the conversation around. We must be able and willing to say "no" graciously. (Phoebe Pelot)

4. Begin with an unexpected, humorous, or startling statement.

Mark Twain said, "It is better to keep your mouth shut and be taken for a fool than to open your mouth and remove all doubt." When we learn to control our tongues, we will not look, sound, or act like a fool. We will also be able to warn and confront, turn the conversation around when needed, and say "no" graciously. (Samara Meahan)

5. Begin with a quotation or familiar saying.

Just say "no," but make sure that you say it graciously. Christians need to learn to treat people kindly and with respect. However, they also must learn to politely decline requests and not over commit themselves. A Christian's speech should glorify the Lord at all times and grace ought to season each sentence they speak. Sometimes Christians face tough situations and must warn or confront. At other times they must change the subject to be sure that their conversations are pleasing to God. (Emily Turner)

6. Begin with dialogue—real or imagined.

"Susie, you don't have time for another class! You're already taking gymnastics, piano, and tennis. You just don't have enough time in your day for all that you want to do."

"But Mom, I already said yes. It's not that I really want another commitment, I just

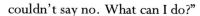

couldn't say no. What can I do?"

Have you ever been stuck in a situation like Susie? Then perhaps you need to learn to say "no" graciously. (Brianna Swanson)

7.   Relate a story or paint a descriptive picture.

A lady sits on the sofa. Her head droops like a wilted flower. Her shoulders shake with suppressed sobs. "I can handle it! I can handle it!" she cries over and over to her cat. Had this lady learned to say "no" graciously, she wouldn't be teaching Sunday school, filling in at the nursery for someone who is sick, providing special music, and doing her regular nursery turn during the evening service. She needs to learn to say "no" graciously.

One Class's Answers
Exercise 7

2.   Ask a question.

Do you like plants? Do you have some spare time? Would you enjoy teaching others basic botany and planting techniques? If so, you might consider volunteering as a municipal garden docent. <u>Many gardens offer docent training programs to equip you to lead tours, identify plants and their origins, and use drought-tolerant plants in your own garden.</u>

Note: Begins with question, in this case, a triple question.

or

Local municipal gardens frequently search for volunteers to give tours of their facilities. In fact, the Bancroft Gardens in Walnut Creek will offer a training class next week. <u>The eight-week program will equip docents to lead tours, identify plants and their origins, and use drought-tolerant plants in local gardens.</u> Is Bancroft Gardens calling you?

3.   Show a benefit to be gained.

Docents at the Bancroft Gardens learn their Latin. Words like *Corydalis solida* roll easily off their tongues. <u>As part of an eight-week class, docents learn to lead public tours, identify specific plants and their pedigrees, and choose drought-tolerant species for their own gardens.</u> Latin instruction comes as an added benefit.

or

Municipal garden docents get to spread their love of plants like the shoots of the bamboo plants they tend.

4.   Begin with an unexpected, humorous, or startling statement.

Cacti from the Sonoran Desert, coffee plants from the slopes of the Andes, and anthuriums from the interior of the Hawaiian Islands all make their home in Walnut Creek, California. Volunteer docents delight to share these exotic plants with thousands of visitors each year. <u>Constantly recruiting help, the gardens offer quarterly classes on leading tours, identifying plants and their origins, and using drought-tolerant plants in local gardens.</u>

or

Stroll through the Bancroft Gardens, but don't wander too far from the path—unless you want to be attacked by a cactus.

or

Docents at the Bancroft Gardens explore their roots.

or

True love is at the root of garden docents' efforts.

5.　Begin with a quotation or familiar saying.

"A rolling stone gathers no moss." The stones at the Bancroft Gardens do not roll, but they are covered with plenty of moss. Among other duties, volunteer docents help visitors enjoy and identify the garden's ten varieties of moss. <u>They learn all kinds of facts in classes designed to equip them to lead tours, identify plants and their origins, and promote drought-tolerant plants in local gardens.</u>

6.　Begin with dialogue—real or imagined.

"People get really excited looking at exotic plants. It's fun and rewarding to share the history of the hundreds of plants thriving at the Bancroft Gardens," said Amanda Stewart, explaining her docent duties at the newly opened municipal gardens. Bancroft Gardens, like other non-profit organizations, relies on volunteers to educate the public. <u>They offer classes to equip docents to lead tours, identify plants and their origins, and use drought-tolerant plants in local gardens.</u>

Note: Writer used an "actual" quote, perhaps obtained from an interview.

7.　Relate a story or paint a descriptive picture.

The morning sun spreads its rays over the Bancroft Gardens, like a mother rousing her sleepy children. California poppies unfurl their golden blooms, and hundreds of roses dispel their fragrant perfume, while docents prepare to share the garden's delights with school children, out-of-town visitors, and even some locals. <u>To equip volunteers, the gardens offer classes on leading tours, identifying plants and their origins, and using drought-tolerant plants in local gardens.</u> In fact, a class begins next week.

One Class's Answers

Exercise 8

2.　Ask a question.

Is oversleeping a problem for you? Monks of the Middle Ages encountered a similar difficulty. To obey the command of Psalm 63:6, "When I remember thee upon my bed, and meditate on thee in the night watches," they needed a reliable way to awaken each night for their prayers. Enter the medieval mechanical clock, the greatest invention of all time. First appearing on cathedrals in the thirteenth century, clocks now appear on every dashboard, wrist, and wall. <u>Providing a reliable way to tell time, clocks drastically impact society and all of life.</u> (Amber Myers)

3.   Show a benefit to be gained.

A lot of people run late these days. It is not only an annoyance to the people who are waiting but also very stressful for the person who is running late. There happens to be a blessing from the Middle Ages that may relieve today's stress: the clock. This clever device can be worn on the wrist or installed in a car. No more late events. This wonderful invention provides a reliable way to tell time. <u>It drastically impacts society and all of life as it relieves stress in today's busy world.</u> (Brianna Swanson)

4.   Begin with an unexpected, humorous, or startling statement.

Without it, life as we know it would cease to exist on planet earth. In fact, recently there was a worldwide panic attack about it. No, not the ozone layer. Clocks. What started as a thirteenth-century device to call monks to prayer has developed into a key part of civilization. Just how important are they? Consider an example. The whole Y2K problem was about tiny clocks inside computers. People were so scared about what would happen when those tiny clocks got confused about the date that many moved to the country and dug bomb shelters. <u>Clocks have drastically impacted our lives in other ways as well.</u> (Cailin Andruss)

5.   Begin with a quotation or familiar saying.

Necessity is the mother of almost all inventions, including the clock. It all started in the Middle Ages when monks found that they needed a reliable timekeeper that would wake them up in time for prayer. The medieval mechanical clock was the solution that began appearing in thirteenth-century cathedrals. <u>Now clocks are everywhere and have drastically impacted our society</u>. (Cailin Andruss)

6.   Begin with dialogue—real or imagined.

"Mom, what time is it?"

It may seem like an ordinary question, but at one point in time there were no clocks. During the Middle Ages, monks had a problem. How could they rise in the night to say their monastic prayers? Inventors came to their rescue with clocks. They first appeared in cathedrals in the thirteenth century but now appear on every dashboard, wrist, and wall. <u>Providing a reliable way to tell time, clocks drastically impacted society and all of life.</u> (Amber Myers)

7.   Begin with description or a story.

The monks of the Middle Ages had a problem. In order to fulfill the required prayers each night, they had to wake up consistently on time. However, they did not have a reliable way to keep time because sundials don't work at night. So they got creative, and the medieval mechanical clock was born. <u>Ever since, clocks have drastically impacted society and all of life.</u> (Cailin Andruss)

And Then . . .

Every now and then I come across an introduction that I just have to clip and save. Since I came across this one while revising these pages, I just had to share it.

> Before it became the single biggest environmental catastrophe in American history, BP's Deepwater Horizon was a magnet for barracudas, which endlessly circled the oil rig in the Gulf's warm waters, feeding on smaller fish. The oil plume and massive clean-up have driven away many of the underwater predators. But as a group of Vietnamese-American lawyers discovered before returning to the Bay Area from the Gulf of Mexico last week, the barracudas have come ashore.
>
> And they were carrying briefcases.

What a wonderful dramatic opening!

Newman, Bruce. "Lawyers Target Unwary Fisherman." *Contra Costa Times* 5 July 2010: A1. Print.

Chapter Six
Conclusions

In many ways, this lesson is a continuation of Chapter 5 on introductory techniques, although conclusions are just a bit less creative than introductions. Since conclusions are the last word, so to speak, it's important to give them the attention they deserve. When students write actual essays, instead of pieces as we've been practicing, they often run out of steam at the end. They've spent so much creativity on their introductions, so much brain power on their thesis statement, and so much stamina on their body paragraphs that by the time they arrive at their conclusion, they're spent. The content of this chapter will help them get a second wind and push for that final burst of enthusiasm.

Pop Quizzes and Entry Cards
1. What is one purpose of a conclusion? (bring essay to a satisfying end, issue a call to action, emphasize the most important point, or tie up loose ends)
2. There are seven kinds of conclusions. Name four. (restate and summarize, question, benefit, humor/startling statement, quotation, call to action, story)
3. What is a dramatic closing? (a tie-in or frame to a dramatic opening)
4. What are two problems with conclusions? (omitting or including too much information)
5. With what two words should you never begin your conclusion? ("In conclusion")
6. What is a frame? (using the same concluding technique that you used in your introduction)

Lesson Specific Issues
➢   Encourage your students to use their concluding technique early in the conclusion, and then move to a concluding line.
➢   Do not begin the concluding paragraph with the words "In conclusion."
➢   Require your student to try *all* of the concluding techniques. You might have to help with content, suggesting a quotation or Bible verse, for example.
➢   Make sure the conclusion makes sense and uses good transitions.

Mini-Lecture & Modeling
In this chapter, you will need to model two types of conclusions: the basic model and the more creative options. Be sure to emphasize the difference between the two and when students should consider using each.

For the basic pattern, model it twice with both a narrative and persuasive topic. Be sure to label each step as you write on the whiteboard, chart paper, or use a pre-made overhead, PowerPoint slide, or Appendix A of the student book, and reveal one point at a time. Next give students a chance to practice with Exercise 9 individually. As students work silently, walk around and read over their shoulders. Either offer individual help or call on students to share. Discuss answers, share the One Class's Answers as necessary, and move on.

The teaching plan for the rest of this chapter is exactly the same as the teaching plan for introductions. This will emphasize the relationship between the two.

Begin by examining the conclusion techniques in the students' books, model them with the suggestions below, and where possible, emphasize the frame or connection with the introduction.

Practice with Help
Also see suggestions for groups in the Teaching Methods section.

Group students into threes or fours, and have them try Exercise 10. Follow the same procedure as you did for practicing introductions. You might even allow students to stay in the same group they were in when they practiced introductions, and have them attempt the corresponding concluding techniques. Alternatively, you might put them into entirely new groups. Either works. What is important is that they have the opportunity to practice and hear all of the techniques and ideas.

On Your Own
Also see teaching suggestions for homework / independent practice in the Teaching Methods section.

Assign Exercise 11 for independent practice. Select some of the students' responses to show as exemplary models or choose from One Class's Answers to Exercise 10. Please note that there is no independent practice for Exercise 9, The Basic Conclusion, since the emphasis here is on the more creative options. Students should know that the basic pattern exists, but they should spend their time practicing the other alternatives.

Modeling
The Basic Conclusion

1.   Narrative Topic: Friendship
Ever since my friend betrayed my trust, I've been more careful with whom I share my innermost thoughts. I think, if this friend shared these comments with everyone we know, would I be OK with that? Often I've stopped or waited until our relationship had stood several tests of loyalty. I've learned that sometimes silence is golden.

2.   Persuasive Topic: Education
Attending college is incredibly expensive, but worth the investment. Planning ahead will lessen the burden as will exploring alternative methods such as online classes, self-study, and credit by exam. Do your research and consider your options. The greatest gift you can give yourself is to graduate debt-free.

Modeling
Creative Conclusions

1.   Broaden out.

Without a doubt, it's hard to say "no." It's even harder to say it with grace. We need to remember the Lord gives us a certain number of hours each day. It's easy to fill up that time with too many activities and become over-committed. We need to guard our time and remember that sometimes saying "no" honors the Lord.

Directions: The above introduction gives some background and states the thesis. Rewrite it using each of the following introductory techniques, and try to include other style techniques you have learned.

2.   Answer or ask a question.

Do you have trouble saying no to people? Of course it is hard to tell people you can't help them, to see their disappointed faces, and to feel that you've let them down. However, as you master saying no with grace, your disappointment will be eased. Remember, sometimes saying no honors the Lord because He has given us a limited number of hours each day to fill wisely. (Brianna Swanson)

3.   Show the benefit gained.

There are so many benefits to saying no, including more time in your day. In many cases it can help you do what is right, and sometimes it can keep you out of trouble. (Bruce Cork)

4.   End with an unexpected, humorous, or startling statement.

Would you be happy if your family was so busy that they found absolutely no time to spend with you? That's how Jesus feels when we're too busy to spend time with Him. So, please just say "no," and He'll thank you for it. (Samara Meahan)

5.   End with a suggested course of action.

Our saying "no" to too many activities honors the Lord. It's hard, but we must remember that the Lord gives help to those who ask. Just ask Him and He'll help. It's easy to fill up the day with so many activities that spark our interest. However, we must remember to guard out time and remember that sometimes saying "no" honors the Lord. Look to fellow believers of Christ for help in this difficult situation. (Amber Myers)

6.   End with a quotation or a familiar saying.

As Ecclesiastes 5:5 says, "It is better that you should not vow than that you should vow and not pay" (NASV). In other words, it's better not to promise to do something than to promise and not be able to do it. Next time, just say "no"—graciously. (Samara Meahan)

7. Finish the story.

What happened to the lady crying on her couch? She finished her cry, got up, and did her best at the tasks she had before her. But next time, she was careful to not bite off more than she could swallow. (Samara Meahan)

One Class's Answers
Exercise 9

1. Topic: Video Games

Although some video games do have their benefits such as providing relaxation, improving hand-eye coordination, and requiring strategic thinking, they also have their downside. Be careful to limit your playing time; monitor it closely. Otherwise you'll look up and find that you've just consumed the past six hours, and you'll wake up the next morning tired, grouchy, and with dark circles under your eyes. And that won't do. After all, you do need your beauty sleep.

One Class's Answers
Exercise 10

2. Answer or ask a question.

There is no question that clocks have shaped modern times. What would we do without them? Well for one thing, we would not have to invent a creative or far-fetched excuse the next time we are late.

3. Show the benefit gained.

Clocks have done more than shape modern life. In addition to helping navigation, furthering the gospel, and promoting business, they have helped me keep my job. My faithful alarm clock jars me awake every morning, just in time to deliver newspapers to everyone on my route.

4. End with an unexpected, humorous, or startling statement.

As 1999 turned into 2000, we sat in out kitchen waiting for the lights to go out and civilization as we knew it to end. But that didn't happen. The lights stayed on and the clocks kept working. Although we were relieved, it might have been nice to be released from the tyranny of time—just for a little while.

5. End with a suggested course of action.

Time is fleeting. Therefore, wasting even one minute needlessly robs valuable time that can never be replaced. The invention of mechanical clocks helped medieval monks redeem the time, and they continue to help us to this day. So impact life. Wear a reliable timepiece and add back those precious lost minutes into your own day.

6. End with a quotation or a familiar saying.

Necessity is the mother of almost all inventions, including the medieval mechanical clock. From navigation on the sea, missions work overseas, and business opportunities on land, this invention continues to be necessary for modern people to function.

7. Finish the story.

The monks of the Middle Ages solved their problem and woke up each night for prayer. Perhaps they were groggy, but they still found time to practice those lovely Gregorian Chants. Not only did they change the course of daily life, they left us some wonderful music.

One Class's Answers

Exercise 11

1. Broaden out.

Television wastes children's valuable time, exposes them to unsavory situations, and encourages them to be sedate. It is harmful. Considering all of the other activities that children might pursue, watching television is a very poor alternative. It dulls the body, the mind, and the soul.

2. Answer or ask a question.

Would Abraham Lincoln have become a great president of the United States if he had whiled away his time watching television? Probably not. Instead, he developed a great mind by reading classical literature by firelight. He used his time wisely, maintained ethical principles, and developed a trim physique from chopping all that wood. And just think, he did it all without *Sesame Street*.

3. Show the benefit gained.

A child who does not watch television could add the equivalent of nine years to his or her life span. These could be healthy years spent pursuing edifying activities. Just think of what a person could accomplish in nine years. He might master a musical instrument, write a novel, minister in his church. Wasting time in front of a box pales in comparison to these accomplishments. Television is a poor substitute for real life.

4. End with an unexpected, humorous, or startling statement.

By the time the average child finishes elementary school, he or she will have witnessed 8,000 murders. Without television, a child might never have that opportunity. Combined with the huge amount of time that it wastes and the unhealthy lifestyle it promotes, television is a poor choice for America's youth.

5.   End with a suggested course of action.

Here's a radical idea: Turn your television off. Better yet, get rid of it entirely. Reclaim that time, cleanse that mind, and drop those pounds. National Turn Off the TV week is nearing. Consider joining millions of Americans who will find something more productive to do with their time.

6.   End with a quotation or a familiar saying.

Comedian Fred Allen once said, "Television is a medium because anything good on it is rare." Instead of settling for something mediocre, children should be encouraged to be active, explore, and exercise their imaginations. Anything less robs them of a fulfilling childhood.

7.   Finish the story.

After my dad gave our TV away, we didn't know what to do with ourselves. It was such a shock. But slowly, over the next month, we adjusted. We took walks, played games, and read books. Now I wonder where we ever found the time to watch TV. Sometimes we miss it, but most days we are too busy doing other exciting things with the new time we have received.

Chapter Seven
Form Review

● ● ● ● ● ● ● ● ● ● ● ● ● ● ● ●

Although not all students will need to do this chapter, all will benefit. Since there has been a period of time between now and when the essay elements were introduced, I like to make sure that all that knowledge is at the forefront of each of my students' brains. Techniques have to be learned before they can be practiced. Therefore, this lesson is almost all review. The only thing that is a little new is the bridge paragraph hook, which students learned about in Chapter 4 but never had the opportunity to practice.

Pop Quizzes and Entry Cards
None for this lesson. Refer to options in previous lessons if desired.

Lesson Specific Issues
  ➢ Be patient! Some students who grasped each individual technique will have trouble putting them together. This will come.
  ➢ Encourage students to try their hand at changing some of Spurgeon's archaic words or rearranging his sentences.
  ➢ Make sure students don't exclusively use the same introductory or concluding techniques.
  ➢ Correct Bible verse punctuation: "The Bible verse" (I Address 11:14). Note that the period occurs after the right parenthesis, not inside the Bible verse's quotation mark.

Mini-Lecture and Modeling
Review the elements of essay structure in as much detail as you feel is necessary. Try to do this quickly as this is not the main emphasis of the lesson, but more importantly, do whatever your class needs. If they haven't reached the place where you want them to be, you need to reteach.

Bridge Transitions
Return to Chapter 4 and the concept of bridge transitions, also called paragraph hooks. Using the model from the student book, explain how to transition from one paragraph to the next using a transitional word, repeating a word, or reflecting a word or idea. When reviewing students' work, or when using the models from these teacher pages, call attention to each bridge transition for emphasis.

Practice with Help
Also see suggestions for groups in the Teaching Methods section.

Since each student has already learned the skills necessary for this lesson, rather than grouping them, allow each to work individually. Assign Exercise 12, and devote a fair amount of class for students to turn the devotion into an essay by themselves. As students work silently, walk around the room, read over their shoulders, and offer help as needed. Make sure students proofread their essays. Some students will finish early. While you are waiting for others to finish, read the fast finishers' essays and offer suggestions for revision.

When all or most have finished, or when you feel students have devoted enough time to this exercise, allow students to pick a partner. Students should read their own essays to their partners, out loud. (This helps with proofreading and allows students to hear what they actually wrote.) The partners should offer at least two and preferably three comments: something done well and one or two suggestions for improvement. Students should record these ideas on their drafts. Then switch and follow the same procedure with the partners' essays. During this babble of voices, walk around the room, listen in on the conversations, and jump in wherever necessary.

After students have shared, you can either ask students to pick a new partner and repeat the process, or ask for someone to nominate an exemplary essay and read it aloud to the class. Before you comment on it, ask what advice the partner offered, and then offer your own. Also, be sure to call attention to and examine bridge transitions.

Finish up by sharing the model for Exercise 12, calling specific attention to the bridge transitions. Use the editing notes to discuss specific organizational and stylistic choices.

On Your Own

Also see teaching suggestions for homework / independent practice in the Teaching Methods section.

Assign Exercise 13 as homework, and assess student progress. Develop a plan to address difficulties, or reteach problem areas. If you don't receive anything you would like to share, use the samples in One Class's Answers to Exercise 13 on page 70.

Modeling
Exercise 12 (Assignment)

Directions: The devotion below was written in the nineteenth century by an English minister, Charles Spurgeon. Turn Spurgeon's devotion into an essay. Write an introduction (with thesis) and a conclusion. Separate the body into paragraphs and provide transitions. Look for repeated phrases or natural breaks and a topic for your conclusion. Give your essay a title.

"Wait on the Lord" (Psalm 27:14)

Sometimes it takes years of teaching before we learn to wait. It is much easier to forge ahead than to stand still. There are hours of perplexity when the most willing spirit, anxiously desirous to serve the Lord, does not know what path to take. Then what will it do? Fly back in cowardice, turn to the right hand in fear, or rush forward in presumption? No, it must simply wait. Wait in prayer, however. Call on God and spread the case before Him. Tell Him your difficulty and plead His promise of aid. In dilemmas between one duty and another, it is sweet to be humble as a child and wait with simplicity of soul on the Lord. It is sure to be well with us when we are heavily willing to be guided by the will of God. But wait in faith. Express your unstaggering confidence in Him. Unfaithful, untrusting waiting is an insult to the Lord. Believe that He will come at the right time. The vision will come and will not tarry. Wait in quiet patience, not rebelling because you are under the affliction, but blessing your God for it. Never murmur as the children of Israel did against Moses. Never wish you could go back to the world again, but accept the case as it is and put it, without any self-will, into the hand of your covenant God, saying, "Now, Lord, not my will, but Yours be done. I do not know what to do. But I will wait until You drive back my foes. I will wait, for my heart is fixed on You alone, O God, and my spirit waits for You in the full conviction that You will be my joy and my salvation, my refuge and my strong tower."

(From *Morning and Evening* by Charles Spurgeon, August 30th.)

"Wait on the Lord" (Psalm 27:14)—Editing Notes

Consequently,

Sometimes it takes years of teaching before we learn to wait. ^ ~~I~~t is much easier to forge ahead than

to stand still. There are hours of perplexity when the most willing spirit, anxiously desirous to serve the

Will it

Lord, does not know what path to take. Then what will it do? ^ ~~F~~ly back in cowardice, turn to the right

hand in fear, or rush forward in presumption? No, it must simply wait. <u>Wait in prayer, however</u>.

your   **You can**

Call on God and spread <u>the</u> case before Him. ^ ~~T~~ell Him your difficulty and plead His promise of

aid. In dilemmas between one duty and another, it is sweet to be humble as a child and wait with sim-

plicity of soul on the Lord. It is sure to be well with us when we are <u>hea~~v~~ily</u> willing to be guided by the

will of God. <u>But wait in faith</u>.

Faith expresses   **rather than**   **which**   **Him**

^ ~~Express~~ your unstaggering confidence in Him.^ <u>unfaithful</u>, untrusting waiting, ^ is an insult to <u>the</u>

                                              Believe that   **(Move to end of**

~~Lord~~. Believe that He will come at the right time. ^ <u>The</u> vision will come and will not tarry. <u>Wait in</u>

paragraph) Do   **those troubles**

<u>quiet patience</u>, ^ <u>not</u> rebel~~ling~~ because you are under the affliction, but bless~~ing~~ your God for ^ <u>it</u>. Never

murmur as the children of Israel did against Moses. Never wish you could go back to the world again,

but accept the case as it is and put it, without any self-will, into the hand of your covenant God~~,~~ sa~~ying~~,

(Save for conclusion)

"Now, Lord, not my will, but Yours be done. I do not know what to do. But I will wait until You

drive back my foes. I will wait, for my heart is fixed on You alone, O God, and my spirit waits for You

in the full conviction that You will be my joy and my salvation, my refuge and my strong tower."

Modeling

Exercise 12 (Essay)

Just Wait

In our modern culture, we hate to wait. We want everything now. With faster Internet connections and cellular phones, we can get immediate access to information and friends. We become frustrated if we have to wait even for a minute. It comes as a surprise and even a shock when the psalmist instructs us to "wait on the Lord" (Psalm 27:14).

Sometimes it takes years of teaching before we learn to wait. Consequently, it is much easier to forge ahead than to stand still. There are hours of perplexity when the most willing spirit, anxiously desirous to serve the Lord, does not know what path to take. Then what will it do? Will it fly back in cowardice, turn to the right hand in fear, or rush forward in presumption? No, it must simply wait. However, wait in prayer.

In prayer you may call on God and spread your case before Him. You can tell Him your difficulty and plead His promise of aid. In dilemmas between one duty and another, it is sweet to be humble as a child and wait with simplicity of soul on the Lord. When we are willing to be guided by the will of God, it is sure to be well with us. But wait in faith.

Faith expresses your unstaggering confidence in Him rather than unfaithful, untrusting waiting, which is an insult to the Lord. Believe that He will come at the right time. Believe that the vision will come and will not tarry. Do not rebel because you are under affliction, but bless your God for those troubles. Never murmur as the children of Israel did against Moses. Never wish you could go back to the world again, but accept the case as it is and put it, without any self-will, into the hand of your covenant God. Wait in quiet patience.

Although our society lacks patience and wants instant gratification, the Lord has bigger plans. He wants us to trust him. He wants us to say, "Now, Lord, not my will, but Yours be done. I do not know what to do. But I will wait until You drive back my foes. I will wait, for my heart is fixed on You alone, O God, and my spirit waits for You in the full conviction that You will be my joy and my salvation, my refuge and my strong tower." The Lord wants us to just wait.

Exercise 13

God's Word Pictures
By Kyle Turner

"Nothing is more indisputable than the existence of our senses" said Jean Le Rond d' Alembert in 1751. In the Bible, God tends to use indisputable experiences in life to show spiritual truths. <u>Faith, in the Scripture, is spoken of as pertaining to all the senses.</u>

"Hear, and your soul shall live" (Isaiah 55:3) shows us that one of the first performances of faith is hearing. We hear the voice of God, not with the outward ear alone, but with the inward ear. We hear it as God's Word, and we believe it to be so. This is the "hearing" of faith.

Faith is also "seeing." "Unto them that look for him shall he appear the second time without sin unto salvation" (Hebrews 9:28). So our mind looks on the truth as it is presented to us that we will understand it and perceive its meaning.

Our perception in faith includes "smelling." "All thy garments smell of myrrh, aloes, and cassia" (Psalm 45:8). We begin to admire Him and find how fragrant He is. This could be called faith in its "smell."

Then, through faith, we appropriate the mercies which are prepared for us in Christ. This is faith in its "touch." By faith the woman came behind and touched the hem of Christ's garment, saying, "If I only touch his garment, I shall get well." In faith, we also handle the things of the good word of life.

Faith is equally the spirit's taste. "How sweet are thy words to my taste! Yea, sweeter than honey to my lips" (Psalm 119:103). "Except ye eat of the flesh of the Son of man, and drink his blood, ye shall have no life in you" (John 6:53). That which gives true enjoyment is the aspect of faith wherein Christ is received into us and made to be the food of our souls. It is then we sit under His shadow with great delight and find His fruit sweet to our taste.

In the Bible, God used pictures of our five senses to teach us His truth about faith. From the sense of hearing, to sight, to smell, to touch, and even to taste, God has shown us what it means to have faith in Him. Senses, the foundation of all human experiences, are one way God uses word pictures to teach us many moral and spiritual lessons.

Spiritual Senses
By Amber Myers

What is faith? The meaning of faith can sometimes be difficult to comprehend, but by comparing it to the five senses, see, hear, smell, touch, and taste, people may come to a better understanding and grow closer to God in the process.

Faith, in the Scriptures, is spoken of as pertaining to all the senses, such as hearing. As it says in Isaiah 55:3, "Hear, and your souls shall live." Therefore, one of the first performances of faith is hearing. We hear the voice of God, not with the outward ear alone, but with the inward ear. We hear it as God's Word, and we believe it to be so; that is the "hearing" of faith. Then our mind looks on the truth as it is presented to us; that is to say, we understand it, we perceive its meaning. This is sight. As it says in Hebrews 9:28, "Unto them that look for him shall he appear the second time without sin unto salvation." So we begin to admire it and find how fragrant it is. That is faith in its "smell." Psalm 45:8 says, "All thy garments smell of myrrh, aloes, and cassia."

Now we appropriate the mercies which are prepared for us in Christ; that is faith in its touch. By faith, the woman came behind and touched the hem of Christ's garment, and by this we handle the things of the good word of life. Equally, faith is the spirit's taste, like the example in Psalm 119:103, "How sweet are they words to my taste! Yea, sweeter than honey to my lips." Also, John 6:53 similarly gives an example of faith's "taste": "Except ye eat the flesh of the Son of man, and drink his blood, ye have no life in you." Christ received into us becomes food for our souls. It is then we sit under His shadow with great delight and find His fruit sweet to our taste.

So what is faith? Faith means being able to understand God's word and to live it, day by day. With the comparison between faith and the five senses, God's children can come to a better understanding and a stronger grip on God's Word with their spiritual senses.

The Five Faith-full Senses

By Samara Meahan

When we, as Christians, learn to live by faith, we are drawn closer to God, and we are able to span some of the distance between our primitive minds and God's omniscient mind. Would you like to know how? Living by faith can be demonstrated by each of our five senses.

Hearing demonstrates faith. "Hear and your soul shall live" (Isaiah 55:3). As one of the first performances of faith, we hear the voice of God, not with the outward ear alone, but with the inward ear. Hearing it as God's Word and believing it to be so is the "hearing" of faith.

Seeing demonstrates faith. After hearing God's Word, our mind looks on the truth as it is presented to us by understanding it, and we perceive its meaning. "Unto them that look for Him shall He appear the second time without sin unto salvation" (Hebrews 9:28).

Smelling demonstrates faith. As we understand God's Word, we begin to admire it and find how fragrant it is. "All thy garments smell of myrrh, aloes, and cassia" (Psalm 45:8).

Touching demonstrates faith. By faith, the woman came behind and touched the hem of Christ's garment. As she did, we can appropriate the mercies which are prepared for us in Christ and handle the things of the Good Word of life.

Tasting demonstrates faith as is seen in two verses: "How sweet are thy words to my taste! Yea, sweeter than honey to my lips" (Psalm 119:103) and "Except ye eat the flesh of the Son of Man, and drink His blood, ye have no life in you" (John 6:53). Therefore, that which gives true enjoyment is the aspect of faith wherein Christ is received into us and made to be the food of our souls.

When we learn to live by faith, draw closer to God, and understand His mind a little more, it is only then that we sit under His shadow with great delight and find His fruit sweet to our taste.

Lesson Reflection & Notes for Next Time

Chapter Eight
Thesis & Outlines

Now that it has had some time to sink in, the concept of a thesis statement should be a little easier for students to grasp. They are ready to move on to some advanced considerations. This chapter presents them. It also gives students some practice using two graphic organizers to organize their thoughts. Since this is the last teaching chapter before students write essays and put what they have learned into practice, review or reteach where necessary.

Pop Quizzes and Entry Cards

1. What is a universal [or superlative or hyperbole]? (a statement that is true all the time [or using words such as *best* or *worst*, exaggeration])
2. With what words might you begin a clausal thesis statement? (when while, where, as, since, if, although. Memory hook: www.asia.)
3. What are the state of being verbs? (is, am, are, was, were, be, being, been)
4. What does *parallelism* mean? (maintaining the same grammatical structure)
5. If I were to ask you to add some "zip" or style to your thesis statement, what would you do? (Use active verbs, strong word choices, and/or careful alliteration.)
6. With respect to prompts, what is the most important thing thesis statements must do? (Answer them.)
7. You should ask four questions when you examine your thesis statements. List two. (Answer the prompt, take a specific position, pass the *how* or *why* test, provide focus.)
8. With respect to thesis statements, what does *qualify* mean? (Limit the circumstances under which the thesis statement is true.)

Lesson Specific Issues

These are the frequent issues my students encounter when writing thesis statements:

> ➢ Relying on a state-of-being or linking verb (is, am, are, was, were, be, being, been): My best friend <u>is</u> _____, _____, and _____.
> ➢ Lacking parallelism
> ➢ For persuasive essays, not presenting a specific argument; thesis statements that do not make a claim
> ➢ Lacking a specific, narrow focus

You might ask students to revisit and improve thesis statements they have previously written or those from Chapter 2, or follow the suggestions below.

Mini-Lecture & Modeling

You will need to model two different topics in this chapter, but thesis statements should take the bulk of your time. Refer to the students' book and discuss thesis issues, clausal thesis statements, parallelism and order, and style. Check to be sure students are taking notes on the note page provided at the end of Chapter 8.

Using the following model thesis statements, discuss their composition and whether they answer three of the four questions. (Since you don't have access to the prompt, most of the time you won't be able to discuss whether the thesis answers it.) Students need to see the thesis statements, so give thought to how you will display them (whiteboard, overhead, chart paper, PowerPoint, handout, or the Modeling Thesis Statements handout located in the student text immediately after the Notes section of Chapter 8).

Here are some ideas to guide your modeling. At first, think out loud as you discuss the deficiencies or strengths of these theses. As you near the end of the problematic examples, involve your class more and solicit their thinking. Even if you don't have enough time to discuss all of the model theses, make sure you end on a positive note by providing some examples of what a quality thesis statement might look like.

Problematic Thesis Statements
1. **TV shows are always terrible.**
   Two problems: Contains a superlative (always) and a state of being verb. Additionally, it is not specific enough: Terrible how? Terrible why?

   Better: Too many TV shows encourage immorality.

2. **There were inconsistencies in the story line because the writers were on strike.**
   State of being verb (were), confusing position (What story line? What writers?), and a fact rather than an argument.

   Better: During the recent writers' strike, story line creativity suffered.

3. **Entertainment is a mind-numbing drug that people use to run away from the world.**
   Not bad. Has some interesting ideas. Tepid verbs though.

   Better: Acting as a mind-numbing drug, entertainment encourages people to abandon their responsibilities.

4. **There were many kinds of programs on the Discovery Channel.**
   State of being verb (were), lacks specificity, confusing position and focus (so what? How does this information apply to the topic? In fact, what is the topic?)

   Better: With the exception of programs on the Discovery Channel, television embraces a wearisome wasteland.

5. **TV is bad, bold, brazen, and boring.**
   State of being verb, wimpy word (bad), maybe a little too much alliteration.

   Better: Viewers need to protest brazen and boring shows.

6. **Movies are usually violent because so many murders and car crashes happen in them.**
   State of being verb (are), wimpy verb (happen), too specific (the number of murders and

crashes would work well for evidence).

Better: Television promotes violence because so many viewers mimic what they see on the tube.

7. **TV shows would be better if producers focused on three things: using less violence, showing less flesh, and to make their writers work harder.**
Good ideas. Would be better if the "be" verb were replaced. Sentence also lacks parallelism (using, showing, to make). "Things" is one of those words that should be banned. It almost always can be replaced with something more specific.

Better: To improve TV shows, producers need to focus on three areas: including less violence, showing less flesh, and making writers work harder.

8. **In our society, everyone blames entertainment for destroying the morals and minds of youth, but in actuality, entertainment is merely a scapegoat for others' failures.**
I like this one. It offers an unusual perspective and piques my interest. I want to read more, which what a good thesis statement should do. It's not perfect, and I would like to see the "our" and "is" changed, but these difficulties are overshadowed by the unique thoughts.

Better: In American society, everyone blames entertainment for destroying the morals and minds of youth, but in actuality, entertainment merely acts as a scapegoat for others' failures.

9. **By touting equality, television builds unity and understanding within communities.**
Fine as is.

10. **Television promotes communication and compassion by exposing society to a variety of common situations.**
Fine as is.

11. **When viewed with discernment, television programs create a smaller and more cohesive world by encouraging people to care and share.**
Fine as is.

Practice with Help
Also see suggestions for groups in the Teaching Methods section.

I firmly believe that students greatly benefit from each other's thinking and discussion, so I frequently conduct a thesis workshop. This is a good place to introduce students to the procedure. Group students into pairs, trios, or quadruplets, depending on the size of your class, and give them class time to evaluate the TV Topic theses in Exercise 14. As they work, all students in the group must agree on one rating for the thesis statement (amazing, excellent, good, lacking) and they must record reasons why as well as improvement suggestions in their book. It's important that all students discuss and write as this promotes engagement.

While students are working, I monitor their discussions and answer their questions, but I also draw a chart on my whiteboard with the number of the thesis statement on the left and columns for each group's opinions to the right. When groups finish collaborating, I give each group a different color marker and invite them to write their findings on the chart. It will look something like this:

Thesis Number	Group 1 (red)	Group 2 (green)	Group 3 (blue)
1	★	★	☺
2	☺	☺	☺
3	☺	√	??
4	??	??	★
5	★	√	??

As students return to their groups, I ask them to put their colored marker somewhere where I can see it so that I can identify which group wrote which column as we discuss the results as a class.

Unless students missed something significant, I would breeze over theses 1 and 2. As long as students substantially agree, that is they are within one level of each other, I'm happy. I might ask students to re-evaluate number 3. First I'd ask the red people why they gave it an excellent, next the blue people why they gave it a lacking, and then the green people which arguments they found most convincing. I'd definitely discuss theses 4 and 5. For one team to give it an amazing and another a lacking is too great of a discrepancy. Either someone missed something or someone saw potential that another missed.

Of course you need to guide the conversation and refocus students when needed, but the students' own discussion of what does and does not make a quality thesis statement will benefit them the most.

On Your Own
Also see teaching suggestions for homework/independent practice in the Teaching Methods section.

Assign Exercise 15 as homework and assess student progress. When checking and discussing students' evaluations, you might conduct another thesis workshop if feasible, or you might choose a couple to discuss as a class. Call on a student to share his or her evaluation, and then ask the rest of the class to agree or disagree and state why. Again, it's the discussion that is most important.

After assigning the Exercises, you may desire to introduce the Graphic Organizers as explained on pages 81 and following of these notes.

Modeling
Thesis Statements

1. TV shows are always terrible.

2. There were inconsistencies in the story line because the writers were on strike.

3. Entertainment is a mind-numbing drug that people use to run away from the world.

4. There were many kinds of programs on the Discovery Channel.

5. TV is bad, bold, brazen, and boring.

6. Movies are usually violent because so many murders and car crashes happen in them.

7. TV shows would be better if producers focused on three things: using less violence, showing less flesh, and to make their writers work harder.

8. In our society, everyone blames entertainment for destroying the morals and minds of youth, but in actuality, entertainment is merely a scapegoat for others' failures.

9. By touting equality, television builds unity and understanding within communities.

10. Television promotes communication and compassion by exposing society to a variety of common situations.

11. When viewed with discernment, television programs create a smaller and more cohesive world by encouraging people to care and share.

One Class's Answers
Exercise 14

For this exercise, it is acceptable to be off by one level, but what is most important is that students can justify their evaluations.

1. From its excessive swearing to its graphic violence, *South Park* represents just one of the many shows on television that negatively influences children.
   ☺ Very solid. Could use just a bit more zip (style).

2. Television has proven to steal time away from more important activities.

    √ Has potential. "has proven to" is not necessary. Would be better to use the verb *steals*. And just what are these "more important activities"? I'd like a preview or hint about how or why TV steals time.

3. Watching too much TV can affect children in negative ways, such as causing childhood obesity, laziness, or even changing children to become violent.

    √ Lacks parallelism (causing, laziness, changing). "In negative ways" lacks specificity—how or why? "Can affect" sounds indecisive. Does it or doesn't it? Good ideas; needs attention.

4. TV is a major distraction to the children in this society and causes them to put off what they are supposed to do.

    √ Verbs are tepid. Lose *is* and use *distract* instead. Instead of "them to put off what they are supposed to do," try *procrastinate*. The result could be: ☺ "TV distracts American children and causes them to procrastinate." Good and solid, but not amazing; that would require greater insight and ideas.

5. Television creates a deceptive world that harms the lives of children.

    ★ See how this one has that greater insight and ideas? I would like to read about how something creates a "deceptive world."

6. Television negatively affects people by producing idle time, illusions about reality, and decreased health.

    √ I'm not too crazy about the verb *producing* and I also don't like the very wide focus (or the three-pronged thesis for that matter). A better essay might focus on one of these topics and develop it. I like "illusions about reality" because that's a little different.

7. Because television causes obsession, exposes children to violence at a young age, and contains program content that can potentially harm children, it is unhealthy.

    √ While the verbs in this one are better in the first clause, they are undone by the "it is unhealthy" in the second. Again, the topic is overly broad.

8. Even though there are several advantages to the television, there are many bad influences that are included.

    ?? This says television is good and bad. It doesn't answer the prompt.

9. Addiction to television will negatively influence children to lie, swear, and perform violent acts.

    ☺ This *might* be a three-prong thesis, but I can't entirely tell without the rest of the essay. Great verbs. Focus seems narrow enough, but again, it's hard to tell. The thesis does pique my interest, and that is what is most important.

10. As a result, television's excessive sexual content poisons children's minds.

    ☺ While I like the verb "poisons," it is almost a cliché. *Pollutes* might work better. Nice narrow topic. The term "as a result" at the beginning is fine and presumably connects this thesis

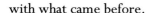

with what came before.

11. Therefore, children's television should be limited because it harms them.
    √   Maybe a good idea, but where is the personality? <Yawn.>

12. Television destroys a minor's adolescence in such a way that children learn violence, lose their innocence, and become less active.
    √   I might be more impressed if the "become less active" could begin with a /l/ sound (but the "less" would have to go; otherwise it would be too much alliteration). Focus is overly broad.

13. The lives of adolescents today are directly influenced by the portrayal of women on TV.
    ??   This is a statement of fact and not an argument.

One Class's Answers

Exercise 15

For this exercise, it is acceptable to be off by one level, but what is most important is that students can justify their evaluations.

1. Although there are some negative effects of advertising, advertising is generally good because it educates people, raises cultural awareness, and causes people to consider helping the world.
    √   Contains a state of being verb ("are"). If it and the word "advertising" were not unnecessarily repeated, I might be more inclined to the ☺, but I'm really not a fan of three pronged thesis statements, especially since there are so many other creative options.

2. Advertising educates the public, informs viewers about their world, and encourages moral actions.
    √   Although it exhibits good parallelism, I'd like to see a narrower focus for the argument. Sentence one lists three topics about one argument. The three in this one don't seem related to each other.

3. The effects of advertising are detrimental if they cause people to be selfish and greedy, but it they cause people to attend to the needs of others, the effects are beneficial.
    ??   Basically, this says advertising is good and bad. It straddles the issue and does not answer the prompt.

4. Ultimately, advertising will bring about negative effects because it sells the wrong products and uses tricky techniques to deceive people into buying the items.
    ☺   Although it could improve grammatically ("product<u>s</u>"), and the word choices could improve ("negative effects" is too general), I'm won over by the word choices and alliteration of

"tricky techniques."

5. It has become blatantly evident that what we wear, what we say, and how we live are determined not by our own set of values but by a set of values instilled upon us by Corporate America.

   ★ Here is an example of the exception to the rule. Although this sentence contains a state of being verb (are), it is still extremely powerful. By using passive voice and saving the words "Corporate America" to the end of the sentence, the student builds suspense—who or what is causing this devastation? "Instilled" is a great verb, and I also like the adverb "blatantly." Some teachers don't like students to use adverbs, but I'm not in that camp.

6. Advertisements enable us to understand the world, and without them we would be devoid of the fundamental abilities of communication and understanding.

   √ This one starts out well but loses me after the word "devoid." Fundamental abilities? Huh? It has potential though. With a bit of a rewrite, it could be strong.

7. Not only do advertisements increase the convenience of daily life, they may also save lives or benefit those in need.

   ☺ Solid. Well-done in terms of ideas. Not enough zip though.

8. The invention of advertising is the best thing that has ever happened to our world.

   ?? Really? And you've looked at every invention ever invented? State of being verb (is), superlative (best), wimpy words (happened and thing), and doesn't say much.

9. Without advertising, many people would be obviously to changes in culture and be left in the dark.

   √ Obviously? Perhaps oblivious? "Left in the dark" is too much of a cliché for me. Thesis has some potential but needs a lot more attention.

10. Advertisers aim for the hearts and minds of men and women, altering their perceptions to create a mentality of soulless commercialism.

    ★ Whoa! I *really* want to read this essay. I'm especially drawn to the phrase "soulless commercialism."

11. Advertising enriches living because it informs people of the latest and greatest effective and time-saving products.

    ☺ I'm not too thrilled with the cliché "latest and greatest," but the rest of the sentence piques my interest.

Graphic Organizers—Modeling & Independent Practice

I have to admit that with more years of school than I care to think about, I never did get the hang of the Roman numeral outline. With the recent trend towards pre-thinking with graphic organizers, I have become more successful. At the end of Chapter 8, two graphic organizers are introduced and should be tried in the next two chapters as students write practice essays. My suggestion is to ask students to use the whole-essay outline for the descriptive essay and the fill-in-the-blanks for the persuasive essay. Students tell me that they really like both of these outlines because they keep them focused on the task at hand.

Practice with Help & On Your Own—Optional Exercises

I don't spend any time practicing graphic organizer use; instead, I just give them to the students to use. If you find yours need more instruction, you have two options.

➢ If you have group time available, group students into pairs, and have them chart the student essay in Exercise 16. Some students should use one organizer and the remainder the other. Select groups to report on their choices, and discuss any issues that arise.

➢ If you run out of group time, and you probably will, assign Exercise 16 as independent practice (homework). If you discover issues, use Exercise 17 to review and reteach.

Students don't usually have trouble with these organizers, so after modeling the organizer, you might move on. However, you know your class best, so if you need more time, be sure to take it.

Modeling

Graphic Organizer #1

_____

　　　Most kids look for a scary monster like Frankenstein or the boogeyman underneath their parents' bed. When I look, I see a humongous collection of cow, kangaroo, alligator, lizard, and even ostrich leather boots all stuffed under my dad's side of the bed. This unique collection happens to belong to my accumulating dad. In addition to his boots, I admire my dad for his honorable character, his culinary skills, and unusual menageries.

　　　My dad's protective character shone when my family drove to Berkeley, and a man unexpectedly punched him. After we got out of the car, we proceeded up the street, searching for the Extreme Pizza restaurant. As we were searching, we became confused because the advertised address for Extreme Pizza was actually a Jamba Juice. Standing there perplexed, we heard, "Don't tell me about the moon!" Hearing this, my father turned around, and immediately, a man slugged my dad in the left eye. The gash bled profusely. The deranged man darted into a nearby book store. Seconds later, two strong, young black men pursued, tackled, and held the man down until the security guard and policeman arrived. Later, we found that the man was bi-polar. I was so proud of my dad for holding his temper and not retaliating. The man couldn't help being ill, and if my dad had punched him back, he could have become more violent and possibly harmed all of us. By displaying fortitude, my dad protected his family.

What kids think is usually under the bed
My dad's collection of boots
Thesis: In addition to his boots, I admire my dad for his honorable character, his culinary skills, and unusual menageries.

▶ **Introduction:** ☐ Funnel ☐ Asks a question ☐ Shows benefit ■ Quotation/saying/startling statement ☐ Dialogue ☐ Tells a story

Thesis: ☐ Informs (states topic) ■ Describes (suggests mood) ☐ Persuades (states position to defend)

■ Academic (three themes with parallelism)

Transition: ■ Bridge transition to first body paragraph

Theme or Topic One Notes

▶

Dad's Character
☐ *Informative: Adds detail, explains and expands theme*
■ *Persuasive: Gives reasons, evidence, examples and illustrations, or quotes*
Pizza trip to Berkeley
Missed location
Altercation
Protective character
Clincher bridges to next topic

Note that "protective character" echoes "honorable character" from the thesis statement.

Modeling

Graphic Organizer #2

Not only will a single-payer healthcare system hurt the economy, but it will also cut the quality of medical treatment. With government paying for healthcare, it will also control what doctors do so that it can save money. This strategy proved to be almost fatal to twenty-eight year-old Melissa Matthews, who lives in the UK, which suffers from universal healthcare. She suspected that she had bowel cancer and had gone through many tests. The doctor said there was nothing to worry about and sent her home. A week later, the cancer reached a critical stage, and Matthews was rushed to the A and E. There, doctors discovered a large tumor in her bowel and were forced to remove her womb and some of her colon. It turns out that the doctor based his diagnosis on government statistics. Statistically, Matthews was too young to have bowel cancer. Statistically, there was a low chance of her having bowel cancer, so the doctor did not bother to do more tests when the first test turned out inconclusive (Donnelly). Basing diagnosis and treatment of a patient on statistics endangers his or her safety. Not every patient is the same. However, doctors in the UK can do little about situations like this since they have to follow government procedures.

Donnelly, Laura. "Patients with Suspected Cancer Forced to Wait So NHS Targets Can Be Hit." *The Daily Telegraph* [London] 7 June 2009, n. pag. Web. 6 July 2010.

Body

Second point or next strongest argument and how it proves the thesis:
Under UHC, quality of medical care will disintegrate

or

Medical care—decrease

Evidence/Support/Showing
UK—already has UHC

Melissa Matthews misdiagnosed

Bowel cancer advanced

A Word About Voice

Although it is beyond the scope of this class, I'd like to take an opportunity to talk about *voice* or the personality behind the words. One of your ultimate goals is to help students discover their writing voice and imbue their essay with personality. If you compare the two essays in Exercises 16 and 17 in the student books, you can illustrate this.

The essay on global warming is filled with personality. You can almost visualize the writer in the room speaking to you. You can hear his voice in your head, and it does sound like a "him," doesn't it? The essay on California's water crisis is more bland. It's informative, persuasive, well-structured, and well-supported. There is nothing wrong with it from a structure and content perspective (which is the focus of this course), but it lacks a voice or personality. It could have been written by anyone, not a specific, unique person.

Voice is the hardest of all the writing components to teach, but I've found that calling attention to it in models sometimes helps. This isn't the time to teach voice, but it is a good opportunity to call attention to it and set up a base for the future.

Lesson Reflection & Notes for Next Time

Chapter Nine
Descriptive Essay

Now it's time for students to practice. Chapters 9 and 10 walk students through the processes of writing a descriptive and persuasive essay. Since students seem to be more comfortable with descriptive writing, it makes sense to start here. As students describe a person, they will develop a thesis statement, body paragraphs with support (showing) and transitions, captivating introductions, and satisfying conclusions. I find that younger students can successfully move on to persuasive essays if they have the opportunity to first write a descriptive essay.

Be very careful to walk your students through each step of the practice essay. Although it might be tempting to let them do it on their own, you will lose most of what you have spent many lessons teaching. Students need to have these points nailed down in their brains. They need your help to make them stick. Think of these last two chapters as "practice with help" lessons. Be sure to offer plenty of guidance. With these two chapters and subsequent essays as well, do not be afraid to offer plenty of suggestions. If your students have too much difficulty formulating a thesis statement, it is perfectly fine to allow them to use one of the examples in this book. It is also perfectly fine to give them one of your own. You are not doing their work for them—you are teaching.

Finally, some students will need to talk about their ideas before they can begin some of the other thinking steps such as asking questions, free-writing, and creating a cluster chart. Encourage them to talk. Draw some ideas out of them. Help start the flow.

Suggested Sequence of Lesson Steps:
Be sure to check students' work frequently.

1. Think about the topic and develop ideas through talking, asking questions, free-writing, and/ or a cluster chart.
2. Develop a thesis. Check it by reviewing suggestions in Chapters 2 and 8. You might also conduct a thesis workshop with students' theses.
3. Using one of the full-essay outlines from Chapter 8, outline the body sections. Think about showing vs. telling.
4. Write the body paragraphs.
5. Check body paragraphs for transitions and revise as necessary.
6. Return to the outline, and think about an appropriate introduction and then a conclusion.
7. Write the introduction and conclusion separately. Refer to Chapters 5 and 6 as necessary.
8. Ask students to proofread their essay by reading it out loud to themselves.
9. Request a rough draft. Evaluate it, reteach as necessary, and give each student specific ideas for improvement.
10. Request final draft.
11. Grade final draft and plan next lesson.

Lesson Specific Issues

➢ Some reminders will be needed for each technique; if students are completely blank on a concept, go back to the chapter where it was taught and review.

Peer Reviews

Peer reviewing has become a very popular teaching technique in recent times, but I am of two minds about its effectiveness. On the one hand, if you have taught your students a model and they understand what a good thesis statement looks like (or body paragraph or introduction or whatever), peer review can have value. Students might give good suggestions for improvement. At certain times during the descriptive essay process, you might be able to use it. On the other hand, I'm not sure it's worth the class time. Too many times I've not seen anything of value come of it, and instead I've also seen new errors introduced. If peer review works in your class-room, by all means use it.

One Student's Answer

Descriptive Essay Example

Laughing uncontrollably, I looked at the clock and noticed it said twelve a.m. Annie and I had just finished watching six movies in a row and couldn't stop giggling. As we finally settled down in our sleeping bags, I couldn't help but think of how we had known each other since first grade and how blessed I was, seven years later, to still have such a great friend. I value my friend Annie because she likes to have fun, acts kindly towards others, and accepts our differences.

Annie and I have had so many enjoyable times together. Summer camp-outs in the back-yard, making candy at Christmas, and doing pedicures at sleepovers are just a few of my favorite memories. One time, while night-swimming in my pool, our "kid-ish" side took over and we started to do the "hokey pokey" for no reason at all. She is not afraid to be silly and enjoy life. I like that. Annie always has a cheery smile and is fun to be with.

Caring and compassionate are two words that describe my friend Annie. She is always kind to my sister, who is a little different than most kids. Many times, when my sister has to go into the hospital, Annie asks her family to "adopt" me, and invites me to stay with her as long as I need to. She is also very supportive and a good listener. She has always been there to talk to, es-pecially when I have been sad about losing pets. Annie helps out whenever she can, especially as a pet sitter, when my family goes away.

One of the most important things about our friendship is that Annie accepts our distinc-tions. Being the same age and grade, we have many things in common. We also have many differ-ent interests. For instance, Annie likes scary movies, and I do not. She goes to public school, and I am homeschooled. Annie likes all kinds of foods, but I do not. Annie likes fantasy books, and I do not. Many kids would let these differences interfere with their friendships. Annie and I do not.

Annie is a special friend. She likes to have fun, acts kindly towards others, and accepts our differences. We met in first grade and have been through so much together. We have grown over the years. I look forward to continuing to grow up together as best friends. (Jenny Schulke)

Chapter Ten
Persuasive Essay

The topic selected for this chapter is really a high school topic and requires research. Some middle-schoolers might have difficulty with it, especially if their access to the Internet has been limited. For these students, you might substitute a different persuasive essay topic. I have had good success with this one: Television: good or bad? Even students who do not watch TV will probably have enough exposure to the medium to form a persuasive opinion. Additionally, since television was the topic of previous exercises (Exercise 18 and the TV Topic Thesis Workshop in the Chapter 9 Lesson Plans), students might have already begun thinking about it. Alternatively, save it for a subsequent persuasive essay topic.

As with the descriptive essay, walk alongside your students as they write their persuasive essay. Suggest topics, allow them to use thesis statements from this book or from you, and talk, talk, talk. Writing is thinking, and you probably will have to stimulate your students' thoughts.

Research

If you want your students to include research and it is new to them, you will probably have to help them. Be sure to plan for this step in your schedule, as it will take more time than you think. Sometimes I pre-select four or five sources for students to use. At other times, I ask students to find their own appropriate research and submit it as a separate assignment, like this:

1. A descriptive title that describes the source's content
2. Source. If a website, the URL: www.source.com
3. Several sentences describing the website's content and how it might be used in a essay

Example:

> Is TV healthy for kids?
> http://kidshealth.org/parent/positive/family/tv_affects_child.html
> This article begins by discussing how many hours of TV children should be limited to each day. Then it talks about the disadvantages of TV for children. Next, the article gives statistics about how much violence children would be exposed to when watching TV. The article concludes with risky behaviors, obesity, how commercials can help in child development, parental guidelines, and how to teach children good TV habits. I might use the statistics to support one of my arguments. The disadvantages include some I hadn't thought of, so I'm going to see if I can find more research on them. The guidelines would make a good call to action in my conclusion.

Requiring this summary has two advantages. First, it separates the thinking and writing steps so that students don't sit down to write their outline only to find they have nothing to write about. Second, it allows you to check the validity of the students' source, especially websites. Students tend to think anything on the Internet is valid, which of course is far from the truth. When students begin to research, I check every one of their sources. Yes, every single one. It is a good teaching opportunity. Tedious and painful, but a good teaching opportunity.

If you have several students writing on the same topic in a classroom or co-op class situation, students can share their research. Ask students to email their sources to you (or another student), collate them, and email the result back to the students. You could also create a Wiki or Google Doc if you're able. By reading the descriptions of each source, students should be able to find the information they need to complete their outlines and write their paragraphs.

Formatting the Works Cited Page

In an effort to divide the work of writing a persuasive essay, depending on how comfortable students are with the research step, you might ask them to format the Works Cited entry at the same time they evaluate their sources. In this case, the Works Cited entry would take the place of the URL hotlink or book or magazine title. Using one of the MLA citation generators listed in Chapter 10, the entry for the above research example would be formatted like this:

Gavin, Mary L, MD, and Dowshen Steve, MD. "How TV Affects Your Child." *KidsHealth*.

Nemours Foundation. Feb. 2005. Web. 2 July 2008.

<http://kidshealth.org/parent/positive/family/tv_affects_child.html>.

Please note that since April of 2009, with the 7th edition of MLA, the URL is no longer required. I like to have it when I check websites, but you may feel different. The following citation is completely acceptable:

Gavin, Mary L, MD, and Dowshen Steve, MD. "How TV Affects Your Child." *KidsHealth*.

Nemours Foundation. Feb. 2005. Web. 2 July 2008.

Frequent errors I see when students format the Works Cited page include the following:

1. The words Works Cited (capitalized) appear at the top of the page, centered. It's not Work Cited (no *s*), it's not bold (**Words Cited**), and it's not underlined (<u>Works Cited</u>). Finally, it is Works Cited, not Bibliography.
2. Only sources that are actually cited in the body of the essay appear on this page. In that way, it differs from a bibliography, which is a list of works consulted.
3. Each entry should be a hanging indent and double-spaced, as above. I've single-spaced other citations in this book to save space, but MLA formatting always calls for double-spacing.
4. If more than one entry appears on the page, they should be listed in alphabetical order according to the author's last name or in the absence of an author, the title of the article.
5. There should be no extra lines between entries.

6. If a URL needs to be broken, break it at a slash (/). Do not allow a word processor to arbitrarily force a break at another position.

These are the major errors I see. I've included a checklist in the student pages so that they can check their own entries for completeness.

Crediting sources and creating a Works Cited page takes a lot of effort. You might want to allow students who are new to persuasive essays to postpone this step to a subsequent essay. It's important to discuss it at some point, however. Otherwise students might inadvertently plagiarize their essays, which includes not citing sources even if the article's exact words are not used or their ideas are paraphrased.

Suggested Sequence of Lesson Steps:
1. Think about topic, and develop ideas through talking, asking questions, free-writing, and/or a cluster chart.
2. Ask students to do some research on their own or to read information from sources you provide.
3. Develop a Works Cited page.
4. Develop a thesis. Check it by reviewing suggestions in Chapters Two and Eight. Perhaps conduct a thesis workshop.
5. Using the fill-in-the-blanks outline from Chapter Eight, outline the body sections. Think about SEE (statement, evidence, explanation) as well as showing vs. telling. **Suggestion:** On the first essay(s) your students write, ask them to provide one set of evidence or support for each paragraph/point instead of two as the outline asks for. When they become more comfortable with the task, ask for a second set of evidence for each point.
6. Write the body paragraphs.
7. Check body paragraphs for transitions and paragraph hooks, and revise as necessary.
8. Revise the Works Cited page as necessary.
9. Return to the outline and think about an appropriate introduction and then conclusion.
10. Write the introduction and conclusion separately. Refer to Chapters Five and Six.
11. Ask students to proofread their essays by reading them out loud to themselves.
12. Students submit rough drafts. Evaluate, reteach as necessary, and give specific ideas for improvement.
13. Students submit final drafts.
14. Grade final draft and plan next lesson.

Lesson Specific Issues
- *Internet* is a proper noun and should always be capitalized.
- Encourage students to use their pronouns correctly, called point of view (POV). The pronouns *you* and *your* can be used when they apply to the reader or the essay's audience. They should not be used to refer to a person in general. The pronouns *we*, *us*, or *our* are inclusive. If the statement applies to everyone reading the essay, inclusive pronouns may be used. If not, they can't.
- Sometimes students are reluctant to do research and need to be persuaded.

Exercise 18

➤ **Socialization/Communication:** The Internet harms social prospects because people do not need to exercise kindness in communication.

➤ **Commerce/shopping/business opportunities:** The Internet destroys local businesses that cannot compete with inexpensive goods easily obtainable from the other side of the world.

OR

➤ The Internet promotes small businesses that can draw customers from all over the world.

➤ **Inappropriate content:** Because the Internet makes inappropriate content commonly available, people become desensitized to violence and filth.

➤ **Education:** The Internet gives teachers headaches because it affords students an easy opportunity to plagiarize.

OR

➤ The Internet expands educational opportunities for students by providing easy access to academic databases and expert instructors.

➤ **Your own idea:** People who purposefully spread malicious viruses and worms ought to be tarred and feathered—or at least prosecuted to the fullest extent of the law.

OR

➤ By providing access to flight, hotel, and tourist information, the Internet makes planning a vacation easy and economical.

Body Paragraph Example

Television Prompt

When it made its debut in the 1940s and 1950s, television was enthusiastically hailed as the solution to family problems. It promised to benefit children most of all. According to an advertisement for Motorola televisions, TV is a "blessing" because it keeps "small fry out of mischief . . . and out of mother's hair." Ironically, the ad also boldly states that "Educators, religious and social workers all agree it can be one of the strongest forces in America for bringing the family together to enjoy good, clean entertainment right in the home" (Motorola). Today's reality could not be further from this fantasy. Rather than bring the family together, television has ripped it apart. It is not unusual for a family of four to be separately watching television programs in four different rooms in the home. As for "good, clean entertainment," except for a few programs designed specifically for children, today's programming with its nudity, swearing, and excessive violence exposes innocent children to the darkness of society. Some say that parents have the responsibility to monitor what their children watch. However, because many of today's children have TVs in their bedrooms, supervision is difficult and enforcement can cause family conflict. Television may have promised to strengthen families, but the reality has fallen far short of the dream.

Motorola. 2 July 2008 http://farm2.static.flickr.com/1346/

742398701_c8c64eb96a_o.jpg. Clipping of an ad from the "Daily News" (unknown city)

dated Tuesday, September 5, 1950.

Lesson Reflection & Notes for Next Time

What's Next?

At this point your student has all the tools he or she needs to continue writing elegant essays, except for the topic, which you will need to provide.

Hints for Assigning a Topic

The more specific you can make your assignment, the more successful your students will be. If your students still struggle with some of the components (thesis statement, introduction, conclusion, transitions, and evidence), choose a topic with which your students are familiar. You might specify the type font as well; otherwise, you might be surprised at the variety of creative fonts and spacing options a group of junior high or high school students will devise—a concern for older eyes.

Topic Ideas:

- Determine whether you would like your students to write a descriptive, informative, or persuasive essay. Generally, descriptive essays are easiest for younger students. They might describe a person, place, or object for example, choosing and developing three relevant characteristics.

- For a persuasive essay, I have profitably used the prompt referred to previously: Is television good or bad? Many students already know a lot about this topic through personal experience and observations.

- For an informative topic, make up a subject-related question. For example, if your students are studying America's War for Independence, you might ask for a summary of a major battle and its effect. You might get even more specific and ask for details, such as the battle's name, who won, casualties, what effect it had on the war, who was in charge, and any notable strategy.

- Assign a "how to" topic on some subject familiar to your student for instance, gardening, caring for pets, playing a sport, or another hobby or interest. Tell your student what you want him to include, like background, how he got involved, how it has benefited him, what he likes best about it, or what he has learned, and perhaps a specific incident (like the time his rabbits won first place at the 4-H fair). Be sure your student knows something about the topic if you don't want him to spend his time on research.

- Ask for an opinion on some issue. If because of time constraints you want to avoid research, make sure your student knows a good deal about the issue. Ideas might include arguments for (or against) field trips, the quality (or inferiority) of a specific book or movie, or whether students should (or should not) work in high school. When your students become proficient, tackle more complex topics such as video games, cloning, stem cell research, or immigration policies.

- Give a general topic—sports, for example—and ask students to form a sports-related question and then answer it, e.g., Should steroids be banned from sports? Has athletes' greed marred sports? Can competitive sports be unhealthy? Do salary caps help teams compete fairly? How might sports help students' academics?

- Another controversial topic about which students seem to have an opinion is File Sharing: Piracy or Profit?
- Use an open-ended question as a topic, perhaps one of the following:
  - If you were to write a letter to the president of the United States, what three things would you say to him and why?
  - What person has had the most influence on your life? How? You must provide at least three examples or effects of this influence. You could also describe this person's character.
  - If you could change any one law, what would it be? Why? You must provide at least three reasons or explanations.
  - Explain why you believe young people should or should not move away from home as soon as they are able to support themselves. Give reasons, details, and examples.
  - If you could take a trip to anywhere in the world, where would it be and why? What is special about this place? What would you do and see?

Evaluation

After your student writes one or two practice essays and you are sure he understands the concepts, you might want to begin evaluating each essay according to some criteria you feel is important. You might create a checklist or a rubric like the examples on the next pages. Assign points to each criterion reflecting its importance to you.

Where do you go from here?

When your student masters essay form and structure, perhaps after several practice essays, then what? Are you done? No, you still have three other parts of writing to address: style, mechanics, and voice. (These were discussed in the Course Overview.)

Structure / Organization

For more advanced models of organization, you might investigate how to use specific types of structures (called *modes*), like cause and effect, comparison and contrast, process, or narrative. You will also have to make sure your students understand what does and does not constitute plagiarism, and reinforce MLA style citation conventions.

Style

Style includes all of those language conventions that make writing sing, such as sentence openers and construction (syntax), word choices such as vivid verbs and concrete nouns (diction), and creativity (dress-ups, decorations, imagery, others). The best resource for teaching style remains *Teaching Writing: Structure & Style* by Andrew Pudewa from the Institute for Excellence in Writing. Check out his materials at <u>excellenceinwriting.com</u>, and incorporate a few stylistic devices into each essay.

Mechanics

If your students struggle with grammar, punctuation, or spelling, you will need to provide instruction and practice. Fortunately, you may choose from many good resources. I recommend students purchase an English handbook, such as the Diana Hacker's *Pocket Style Manual* or the even better *A Writer's Ready Reference,* to answer those pesky grammar questions.

Voice

This last section of writing is the most difficult to teach. You will need to approach it from two directions. First, practice, practice, practice. The more essays your students write, the better their expression will become. Second, read quality essays and talk about what makes them work. You might use an anthology or collection of essays, or keep your eye on the newspaper or magazines. When you find something worthwhile, examine it with your students.

Lesson Reflection & Notes for Next Time

STYLE

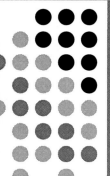

IEW Essay Model & Style Techniques

Basic Essay Model & Style Review

The Elegant Essay is about structure (form or organization) and content (ideas). To profitably use it, students do not have to have any background in the other three essay areas such as style (syntax/sentences, diction/word choice), mechanics (grammar), or voice (personality or overall expression).

On the other hand, many of them already have some background, and you don't want them to lose it.

If you have taught or if your students have taken previous structure and style lessons from the Institute for Excellence in Writing (IEW), you may want to review the basic essay model and the style guides before beginning *The Elegant Essay* lessons. Additionally, your students should keep practicing what they have learned as you do the exercises and write the essays asked for in this book. You know the trite and redundant saying: Use it or lose it.

To review the basic essay model, *The Elegant Essay* teachers (and students) may listen to the following audio file for free. To access the talk go to

excellenceinwriting.com/downloads

Choose the link that says "Redeem your coupon here."

Select < Developing the Essayist > from the drop down menu.

The password for this e-book is *dove*.

Some review of the style guidelines appear on the pages that follow in this appendix.

The Game Is Over

One important thing to remember is that students *do not* need to include all of the style techniques in every paragraph as they did when they were learning them. For example, they do need to use a variety of sentence openers. They do not need to use each of the techniques in every paragraph. Students should use the style techniques they've learned when they fit the students' purposes. Otherwise, their writing will sound formulaic. If you have previously insisted that students include something like all six sentence openers, two dress-ups, and one decoration in each paragraph, it's time to modify those instructions.

Learning the Basic Essay Model & Style Guidelines

Perhaps all of this might be new to you. Not to worry; as I said, this book will teach you what you need to know about structure and content.

On the other hand, the IEW materials are outstanding and will greatly benefit your students. The course you want to look at is the *Student Writing Intensive Level C*, available here: excellenceinwriting.com/sid-c. It is a great beginning to the basic essay model and style techniques, and you might pursue it either before or after this course.

IEW Style Reminders

Dress-Ups—use as necessary

1. *who-which* clause
2. "-ly"
3. *because* clause
4. strong verb
5. quality adjective
6. *when, while, where, as, since, if, although* clause

(Advanced: dual adverbs, verbs, adjectives; noun clause; adverbial or adjectival "teeter-totters")

Sentence Openers—use often

1. subject
2. preposition
3. -ly
4. ing,
5. clausal (www.asia.bu)
6. VSS (very short sentence)
7. advanced: "-ed"

Decorations—use sparingly

1. question
2. conversation
3. 3sss
4. dramatic opening—closing
5. simile—metaphor
6. alliteration

Triple Extensions (Advanced)—use sparingly

1. word repetition
2. phrase & clausal repetition
3. repeating "-ings," consecutive or spaced
4. repeating "-lys," consecutive or spaced
5. repeating adjectives or nouns
6. repeating verbs, consecutive or spaced

-ly Adverb List

abruptly
absently
absentmindedly
accusingly
actually
adversely
affectionately
amazingly
angrily
anxiously
arrogantly
bashfully
beautifully
boldly
bravely
breathlessly
brightly
briskly
broadly
calmly
carefully
carelessly
certainly
cheaply
cheerfully
cleanly
clearly
cleverly
closely
clumsily
coaxingly
commonly
compassionate-
ly
conspicuously
continually
coolly
correctly
crisply
crossly
curiously

daintily
dangerously
darkly
dearly
deceivingly
delicately
delightfully
desperately
determinedly
diligently
disgustingly
distinctly
doggedly
dreamily
emptily
energetically
enormously
enticingly
entirely
enviously
especially
evenly
exactly
excitedly
exclusively
expertly
extremely
fairly
faithfully
famously
fearlessly
ferociously
fervently
finally
foolishly
fortunately
frankly
frantically
freely
frenetically
frightfully

fully
furiously
generally
generously
gently
gleefully
gratefully
greatly
greedily
grumpily
guiltily
happily
harshly
hatefully
heartily
heavily
helpfully
helplessly
highly
hopelessly
hungrily
immediately
importantly
impulsively
inadvertently
increasingly
incredibly
innocently
instantly
intensely
intently
inwardly
jokingly
kindly
knowingly
lawfully
lightly
likely
longingly
loudly
madly

marvelously
meaningfully
mechanically
meekly
mentally
messily
mindfully
miserably
mockingly
mostly
mysteriously
naturally
nearly
neatly
negatively
nervously
nicely
obviously
occasionally
oddly
openly
outwardly
partially
passionately
patiently
perfectly
perpetually
playfully
pleasantly
pleasingly
politely
poorly
positively
potentially
powerfully
professionally
properly
proudly
quaveringly
queerly
quickly

quietly
quintessentially
rapidly
rapturously
ravenously
readily
reassuringly
regretfully
reluctantly
reproachfully
restfully
righteously
rightfully
rigidly
rudely
sadly
safely
scarcely
searchingly
sedately
seemingly
selfishly
separately
seriously
sharply
sheepishly
sleepily
slowly
slyly
softly
solidly
speedily
sternly
stingily
strictly
stubbornly
successfully
superstitiously
surprisingly
suspiciously
sympathetically

tenderly
terribly
thankfully
thoroughly
thoughtfully
tightly
totally
tremendously
triumphantly
truly
truthfully
understandably
unfairly
unfortunately
unhappily
unwillingly
urgently
usually
utterly
vastly
venomously
viciously
violently
warmly
wearily
wholly
wildly
willfully
wisely
wonderfully
wonderingly
worriedly

-ly imposters
chilly
friendly
ghastly
ghostly
holy
kingly
knightly
lonely
lovely
orderly
prickly
queenly
surly
ugly
worldly
wrinkly

Preposition List

aboard	by	over
about	concerning	past
above	despite	since
according to	down	through
across	during	throughout
after	except	to
against	for	toward
along	from	under
amid	in	underneath
among	inside	unlike
around	instead of	until
aside	into	up
at	like	upon
because of	minus	with
before	near	within
behind	of	without
below	off	
beneath	on	
beside	opposite	
between	out	
beyond	outside	